ECHOES

OF THE

MERSEYSIDE

BLITZ

NEIL HOLMES

PEN & SWORD
HISTORY

This book is dedicated to the memory of all those who were killed during the Blitz on Merseyside, may they rest in peace.

First published in Great Britain in 2017 by
Pen & Sword History
An imprint of
Pen & Sword Books Ltd
47 Church Street
Barnsley
South Yorkshire
S70 2AS

ISBN 978 1 52670 258 6

A CIP catalogue record for this book is available from the British Library.

Typeset by Aura Technology and Software Services, India
Printed and bound in India
By Replika Press Pvt. Ltd.

Pen & Sword Books Ltd incorporates the Imprints of Pen & Sword Books
Archaeology, Atlas, Aviation, Battleground, Discovery, Family History, History, Maritime, Military, Naval, Politics, Railways, Select, Transport, True Crime, Fiction, Frontline Books, Leo Cooper, Praetorian Press, Seaforth Publishing, Wharncliffe and White Owl.

For a complete list of Pen & Sword titles please contact
PEN & SWORD BOOKS LIMITED
47 Church Street, Barnsley, South Yorkshire, S70 2AS, England
E-mail: enquiries@pen-and-sword.co.uk
Website: www.pen-and-sword.co.uk

CONTENTS

ACKNOWLEDGEMENTS

The majority of the wartime photographs of the Birkenhead area are reproduced with the kind permission of the Birkenhead Reference Library which holds the copyright for them. Most of the photos of Bootle come from the Stewart Bale Archive, which helped in tracing the organization that originally commissioned the images. This turned out in almost every case to be the Bootle Corporation. These images are therefore reproduced with permission from South Sefton Library Service which holds the copyright for them. They also hold the copyright for the photographs from the Crosby area.

Most of the photographs of Liverpool are the copyright of the Liverpool Record Office which kindly gave permission for their use in this book. Most of the Wallasey photographs are reproduced with permission of the Wallasey Reference Library which holds the copyright for them. I would like to thank the staff at all of the aforementioned establishments for their advice and help in locating information. Once again, I am indebted to Julia Hoffman for compiling the index. My parents have also offered support, and their suggestions have proved to be invaluable. The fantastic support and patience of all at Pen and Sword has also been most welcome.

I have attempted to locate the copyright owner for the historical images on the following pages without success, but would be pleased to hear from them so that proper acknowledgements can be made: pages 8, 24, 39, 44, 46 (both), 73 (lower), 78 (lower), 95, 96, 98 (both), 101 (lower) 102 (both) 103, 104 (both), 110 (upper), 127 (upper) and 155.

There are also a great many people whose help, support and advice has been absolutely essential in recent years. It would be impossible to list all of them here, but I particularly want to thank Dave Jones, Bob Edwards, Sue Kirtlan, Keith Jones, Ken Clark, Ant Hogan, Dave Owens, Dan Longman, Dave Chesworth, Nick Stone, Alan Clay, Dave Bridson, Angie Forshaw, Craig Smith, Caroline Bunford, Phil Bunford and many others.

I also owe a great debt to my partner Tina, who has provided constant support and patience throughout the process.

Author's Note

Since the publication of my first two books, several new sources of information have come to light about The Blitz. Wherever possible, I have attempted to update readers with the correct information in this publication.. This book also represents a snapshot in time, as several of the locations mentioned were undergoing change during the course of my research. For the most part, I have used modern photographs that were up to date at the time of printing, but inevitably views change as the region undergoes development.

If you as a reader, have spotted something you believe be incorrect, please feel free to contact me via my publisher, Pen & Sword. I also invite people to follow me on my Facebook page, and to share any experiences they or their family may have of the blitz, or to ask any questions that are not covered here.

Facebook: https://www.facebook.com/Liverpoolblitz

INTRODUCTION

It has now been six years since the publication of my first book, *Liverpool Blitzed, 70 Years on* (2011), and five since *Merseyside Blitzed* (2012) came out. People might legitimately ask why a third volume is necessary, since the region was already covered by these two works. To be valid in its own right, each new book must bring something new, whether that be new photographs, new information, or a view of the subject from an unexplored angle which sheds new light on it.

This book contains aspects of all three. Although most of the wartime photographs included appeared in the first two books, they are presented here in a different format. Shortly after the publication of my second book, I came across the excellent work of Nick Stone, a graphic designer and photographer based in Norwich. The city of Norwich suffered a series of air raids during the Second World War, with the Baedeker raids of April 1942 being particularly destructive. Nick created a series of amazing images that he called Blitz Ghosts by merging the wartime photograph with a modern one taken on the same spot.

I was instantly struck by how effective this method was, as it created one seamless image conveying exactly where the damage had occurred and its extent. After a lot of help and advice from Nick, I was soon able to create my own images, the first being that of Gray Street in Bootle (seen on page 25). Each image took a lot of work, as it was necessary to find almost exactly the same spot as the original photographer. Once you had the modern photograph, it still required manipulation on the computer to achieve a ghost image, but the results were always worth the effort.

It occurred to me that many of the books about the blitz on Merseyside deal with the events by talking about what happened in just one area. One book may cover raids on Liverpool, whilst another focuses on Bootle, with very little crossover. Very rarely does a book provide a timeline for the whole region, tying together a chronicle of all the major events in one volume. Before I compiled this book, I gained access to two major sources of information about The Merseyside Blitz; the Home Security Information Files, and a volume of the Liverpool ARP reports covering December 1940 up to the end of the May Blitz, both recently rediscovered by local archives.

The idea for this book was therefore born, with the aim of further increasing people's knowledge of the Merseyside Blitz by combining the timeline and photographs. It has taken nearly two years to pull together enough photographs to make this title possible. Not all of the photographs have a specific date recorded for them, but in these cases I have tried to include them at the most logical point in the timeline. It is my hope that you will enjoy the book and remember those who experienced the events first-hand, whether they were victims of the air raids, or survivors. To these people and their generation, we owe the freedoms which we often take for granted.

Most of the book was researched and written between 2013 and 2014, however due to a change of publisher some parts were rewritten and the photography was redone in 2016. This region is constantly changing, but it is critical that we remember the history that led us to this point.

THE EARLY RAIDS,
JULY TO NOVEMBER 1940

Despite the fears of many, although war broke out in September 1939, it would be almost a year before bombs began falling on Merseyside with any frequency. This gave valuable time for the authorities to build up the civil defences in each borough, constructing air raid shelters, requesting volunteers for organizations such as the Auxiliary Fire Service and Air Raid Precautions. There was also time to train them, acquire important equipment and iron out any problems in the system.

Sadly the delay also had some negative effects, as many children who had been evacuated just before war broke out actually returned to their normal homes, often not long before the raids began. A degree of complacency also set in for some, but for most this peaceful period must have been welcome. The people of the region could read about the horrors of the war on the continent in the papers, or see newsreel footage of it in the cinemas, and many would have had no desire to experience it first-hand.

This calm could not last though, as the Luftwaffe had already bombed civilian targets such as Warsaw and Rotterdam, and their attention soon turned to Britain and ports like Liverpool. Starting sporadically at first in late July, before increasing in frequency from late August, the Luftwaffe started pounded the area relentlessly, with night after night of raids. Some of these were only relatively minor affairs as you will see, and although the strain never broke the will of the local people or the resources of the civil defences, the continual hammering must have been extremely stressful, even for those not directly affected by the bombing.

While most of the raids that took place in September 1940 were minor in comparison to those of the Christmas, March or May Blitz, the fact that there was a raid somewhere on Merseyside on no less than twenty-six out of thirty nights that month must have been extremely difficult to cope with. The only advantage these regular but relatively minor raids gave the authorities was a chance to evaluate their responses and make changes where necessary.

Although October and November saw a slight dip in frequency, the ferocity of the raids increased, with heavy damage and loss of life becoming more common. The enemy were also using larger and more complicated devices, including parachute mines and explosive incendiaries. This culminated in the night raid of 28 November 1940, when more than 250 people lost their lives in Liverpool alone, with perhaps as many as 180 of these deaths occurring at a single incident at Durning Road in the Edge Hill area of the city.

With many prominent buildings such as Liverpool's Custom House and Wallasey's Town Hall hit, and most areas of the region bombed, people may well have wondered if things could get any worse.

A very common sight at the start of the war was for public buildings to have their ground floor windows and doorways protected by a wall of sandbags. It was hoped that this would protect it from damage caused by flying debris and shrapnel. This was not possible for all buildings, but two of Liverpool's finest buildings – the Town Hall and the headquarters of the private bank, Martins Bank were certainly considered important enough to warrant the protection. The Town Hall would be badly damaged during the raids, and we are fortunate that this ornate building, the second oldest in the city centre survived.

28/29 JULY 1940

Three bombs fell in fields near Boundary Farm in Thurstaston, one fell in a field near Irby and two fell in fields near Wood Lane in Neston. A nearby building called Woodcote saw slight damage to the roof and windows. At the time it housed officers' quarters for a part of the 38 (Welsh) Division.

8/9 AUGUST 1940

The first serious air raid on Merseyside resulted in its first fatality as a stick of six bombs fell on Prenton, killing a maid called Johanna Mandale who was asleep in a house on Prenton Lane. Other roads hit include Acrefield Road, Burrell Road, Mount Wood Road, Tower Road and Waterpark Road.

10 AUGUST 1940

This proved to be Wallasey's first experience of air raids, with bombs striking Adelaide Street, Cliff Road, Field Road, Gorsey Lane, Ingleby Road, Mill Lane, East Street, Stroude's Corner, Rake Lane, Palatine Road, St George's Mount, Linwood Road, Wheatland Lane, Grosvenor Street, Lily Grove and Tulip Grove. There was a total of thirty-two casualties (six of them fatal) and many properties suffered considerable damage.

Children and adults congregate around numbers 9 to 11 Palatine Road, Wallasey probably eager to catch a glimpse of what was then an entirely novel sight in the borough.

These shops in Rake Lane were damaged in Wallasey's first air raid on 10 August 1940. Most of the windows, especially on the upper floors have been blown out. The corner on the left is still often called Stroude's Corner after a shop which once stood there.

Number 2 Adelaide Street, Wallasey looks slightly different to most of the other properties in the street, leading some to assume that it may have been a post-war creation, built on a bomb site. In fact, it was definitely pre-war as this image shows. The house suffered relatively minor damage in the air raid on the night of 10 August 1940. The street would be hit again later in the raids (see page 76).

17/18 AUGUST 1940

The first bombs fell on Liverpool's built up areas in a raid that lasted less than two hours. A total of twelve bombs were dropped, mostly on the city's south docks. The police reports stated that Brunswick, North Coburg and South Queen's Dock were all hit, whilst Brunswick Goods Station and a grain silo were also struck. Although not named, a ship was also overturned in one of the docks.

19/20 AUGUST 1940

Incendiaries fell on the Eaton Road district of Liverpool, but locals were fortunate that most landed on open ground. Small fires were started in the Robert Davies Nursing Home and nearby houses. Damage was fortunately limited, although two men were reported as slightly injured.

Over on the Wirral, six high explosives landed in a field opposite the Thingwall Garage on Barnston Road, but apart from breaking some of the windows, little damage was done.

More examples of the damage done to Adelaide Street, Wallasey during the air raid on 10 August 1940. This image shows damage to numbers 5-9, looking towards the junction with Mostyn Street. William Huston was killed at number 7. Push bikes were a popular means of transport in wartime because of petrol rationing.

28/29 AUGUST 1940

A serious raid on the region, with a large number of high explosive and incendiary bombs scattered across the area. The Church of St Matthew and St James in Mossley Hill, Liverpool was badly damaged by high explosives, whilst houses in Kingsmead Drive and St Anne's Road were also damaged. A shelter on the corner of Mossley Hill Road and Elmswood Road was hit, with reports that people were trapped. Two petrol tanks in St Mary's Road were also set on fire.

In Crosby, six high explosives and an oil bomb fell to earth. Fortunately for the residents, these first bombs did little damage, either landing in fields near Windermere Road, or on a timber yard. Some incendiary devices also landed in the borough of Birkenhead, although little damage was done, suggesting that they fell in a less populated area.

29 AUGUST 1940

King George VI and Queen Elizabeth paid a visit to Birkenhead during the day. Their tour included a visit to the Cammell Laird shipyards.

Two images of the light damage inflicted on Waterpark Road, Prenton during the raids on Birkenhead. Unfortunately, the original images are undated, but the road was hit during these early raids.

These two houses are next door to each other; above is number 3, called 'Norcroft', whilst left is number 1. called 'Oakdene'.

29/30 AUGUST 1940

Gas and water mains were damaged in several areas of Liverpool during this raid. In the Aigburth, Cressington and Grassendale areas, high explosives and incendiaries started several fires. In most cases, these appear to have been brought under control although one large house in Beechwood Road in Aigburth was badly damaged.

Locations hit by high explosives included Green Lane (off Menlove Avenue), Garrick Street (a house was demolished) and Woodrock Road. On the Dovecot Estate, three Anderson Shelters were hit while an unexploded bomb would later be found at the Hunts Cross Hotel on Hillfoot Road.

This night was also Bootle's first experience of bombing, with incendiary bombs scattered across the borough. The Aintree Road area was particularly badly hit, but no casualties were recorded.

In Crosby, seven high explosives were spread across the borough, killing three people and injuring two.

30/31 AUGUST 1940

This night was the first substantial raid, with bombs falling in all the boroughs closest to the Mersey. Liverpool was hit hard, with bombs landing on the Mill Road Hospital, Coburg Dock, Sefton Street, Brodie Avenue and the Everton district.

Bootle escaped fairly lightly, with only a scattering of incendiaries across the area between Irlam Road and Queen's Road.

Crosby suffered further, with five deaths and six injuries; two houses were demolished and seven badly damaged. High explosives landed in Mason Street, Wesley Street, Albert Road and York Street. Incendiaries were also scattered across the borough.

York Street in Crosby was one of the roads struck during the raids on the night of 30/31 August 1940. This area has changed a great deal since the air raids. The large building to the right of centre, which was known as the Queens Hotel (later called The Waterloo) was still standing when this photograph was taken, but has since been demolished and replaced by housing. It appears to have been the last pre-war building at this end of the street.

Birkenhead was hammered, with bombs hitting Noctorum Road, North Road, West Road, Bidston Road, Howbeck Road, Ingestre Road, Golf Links Road, Waterpark Road, Albany Road, Bedford Road, Morecroft Road and New Chester Road. Wallasey was hit by large calibre high explosive bombs and incendiaries, and the main roads hit were Greenwood Lane, Byerley Street, Elleray Park Road, Earlston Road, Bell Road, Mount Pleasant Road, Shakespeare Road and Stoneby Drive. Casualties in Wallasey were remarkably light, with only one woman slightly injured. Unexploded bombs were later found at Rake Lane Cemetery and in Elleray Park.

In Bebington, a high explosive bomb did extensive damage to Wirral Grammar School Hall, whilst some incendiaries also landed on Unilever's works in Port Sunlight.

31 AUGUST/1 SEPTEMBER 1940

Another heavy night raid battered the region, with fatalities and injuries in most boroughs. Liverpool suffered serious damage from high explosive and incendiary bombs. The Custom House was hit for the first time, setting it on fire. Only the brave and prompt action of the Fire Brigade confined the flames. Cleveland Square saw heavy damage, especially at the end closest to its junction with Pitt Street. A shelter in the square was also hit by a high explosive bomb, causing sixteen deaths. The overhead railway near James Street, was also hit, along with Queens, Coburg, Brunswick and Wapping Docks.

Other targets in the city that night included two cotton warehouses and their contents (presumably consumed by fire) one on Stone Street and the other on Vandries Street. Warehouses in Shaw's Alley, Hurst Street, Kitchen Street, Caryl Street and Sephton Street were also set ablaze. Several bombs landed in the Edge Lane area, damaging houses and a factory, whilst around twenty people were injured near Canning Place and the Gordon Smith institute.

ARP Workers look down from the upper floor bay window of 92 Downing Road, where Elsie Smith was killed on the night of 31 August/ 1 September 1940. No clear trace of the damage remains today.

In Bootle, bombs fell through the night on Bedford, Clare, Downing, Gonville and Sidney Roads, demolishing houses in each. At 92 Downing Road, Elsie Smith was killed, just one of the six fatalities that the borough would suffer that night. Twenty-eight people were injured in the raid.

Houses in Sidney Road, Bootle torn apart by a high explosive bomb on the night of 31 August/ 1 September 1940. The properties with the heaviest damage here are numbers 70 and 72.

Number 55 Clare Road, Bootle. This photograph dates from the aftermath of the night of 21/22 September 1940 when the road was also hit. Despite being from another raid, it gives some idea of what kind of damage may have been done during the earlier night's action.

Above: Two more examples of the damage done on the night of 31 August/1 September 1940. The photograph above was originally thought to show Sidney Road and featured in my second book as such, but further research has revealed it to actually show Gonville Road, with the heaviest damage being done to numbers 74 and 76. Gonville and Sidney Roads are in fact parallel to each other.

Left: Bedford Road, seen from the junction with Southport Road. The house on the corner is number 272 Bedford Road.

Two minor incidents occurred in the borough of Crosby overnight, first four high explosive bombs landed in the sand dunes near Hightown. They came to earth between a searchlight station and the fort, but did very little damage. This was fortunate, because during the war the fort was an important part of the region's defences, although it was never called into action. It did however examine shipping heading for Liverpool and the Wirral, a role it shared with Fort Perch Rock in New Brighton.

Almost two hours later, a single high explosive landed in the front garden of 17 Adelaide Terrace, doing minor damage to the property and nearby walls.

In Wallasey, the area around the town hall was particularly badly affected with Littledale Road, Dock Road, Brighton Street, Bell Road, River View, Church Street and Falkland Road all hit. The town hall suffered heavy damage to its south western corner, battering the organ and concert hall.

Adelaide Terrace, Waterloo seen shortly after the raid mentioned above. Wartime workers dig holes in the modern pavement.

Wallasey Town Hall, as seen from Brighton Street shortly after the raid on the night of 31 August/1 September 1940. Workers are already present, attempting to clear the damage from this major road. The damage done to the town hall itself would likely take much longer to repair. The King and Queen would be photographed outside the hall during their visit in November 1940.

Meanwhile, in Birkenhead, incendiary bombs began to rain down on the borough just before 9.00 pm, with high explosive bombs following closely on their heels. The damage was widespread and extensive, with numerous locations in Rock Ferry, Bidston, Tranmere, Noctorum and the town centre hit.

One of the bombs landed near the battleship HMS *Prince of Wales*, between the ship and the quayside in Cammell Laird Shipyards. The warship, which was still under construction at the time, was damaged in the explosion, which buckled her armoured hull. Through the hard work of the nearby firefighters and shipyard workers, the water which flooded the ship was eventually pumped out and the vessel was repaired. The damage caused a slight delay in her being commissioned.

At least four people were killed in Birkenhead and a large number were seriously injured.

The far side of Brighton Street, showing damage done near the Brighton Hotel. This block lies between Bell Road (left) and Buchanan Road. At the time of writing, the Brighton Hotel (the turreted building) is closed.

Two men from the civil defences converse, presumably about the damage done to these properties in the Dacre Hill area of Rock Ferry. A high explosive bomb has all but destroyed the property they are standing near, whilst doing enough damage to the building on their left to warrant its demolition. All that stands there now is two modern advertising hoardings. The building on the right was a fish and chips shop during the war.

A man stands on the roof of a property on the corner of Bebington Road and Bedford Drive, perhaps surveying the damage which occurred on the night of 31 August/ 1 September 1940. Compared to other locations in Birkenhead, the damage was slight. Meanwhile, in the twenty-first century. a man walks his dog, probably oblivious to the damage he would have seen had he been on a similar trip a little over 70 years before.

2 SEPTEMBER 1940

A minor raid as bombs stuck the borough of Bebington once more. Incendiary bombs fell near the southern boundary of the borough, and in the Woodhey area, but did little damage. Six adults were slightly injured in the raid. An unexploded bomb was found on the Chester to Birkenhead line near Bebington Station, but was dealt with. Houses, a pub, shops and a cinema were also reportedly damaged by seven high explosives which fell on the New Ferry area. High explosives also landed on Poulton and Brimstage.

3/4 SEPTEMBER 1940

Bombs rained down on several different areas of Liverpool, including high explosive bombs in the Kensington, Lark Lane and Ullet Road areas. Incendiary bombs landed on Aigburth Vale High School and Lodge Lane Rope Works. One of the other victims of the night's raid was the Palace Ice Rink in Kensington.

Meanwhile over in Bootle, a single bomb was reported as landing on a warehouse in Howe Street, damaging a ground floor gable in the building, partially demolishing a house opposite and damaging several more nearby. An ARP warden was awarded the British Empire Medal for his gallantry during the raid. He came across a number of people hiding underneath a bed, below a ceiling that was due to collapse from the damage. He supported the ceiling on his bent back just long enough for the civilians to escape, barely getting out of the building himself before the ceiling caved in for good.

A total of six high explosive bombs were scattered across the Crosby area, mostly landing in fields, gardens or the rear of houses in the early hours of the morning of 4 September. Two oil bombs landed in the grounds of Merchant Taylors' School in Crosby.

Two bombs fell on Heswall, starting a minor fire.

4/5 SEPTEMBER 1940

During this raid a series of high explosive bombs landed on the Edge Hill and Lister Drive areas of Liverpool. The authorities believed that the goods station at the former and the power station at the latter were the most likely targets, although neither was actually hit. Instead the bombs fell on surrounding properties, while other bombs landed on the Dunlop Rubber Works and the Tunnel Road Cinema. Initial reports cited twelve dead and thirty-four injured, although as this was a regional report including details of the Bootle raid, these figures may not be for Liverpool alone. Damage was also done to areas of Langton, Alexandra and Brocklebank Docks and several people were reported trapped in Walton Village.

In Bootle, bombs rained down on the borough, killing one person and injuring thirty-nine others in a raid that lasted for more than six hours. Houses were damaged in Strand Road East, Elm Street, Cedar Street, Stanley Road, Marsh Lane, Malta Road and Ibstock Road.

The Salvation Army Barracks building on Stanley Road in Bootle showing some of the damage done during the raid on the night of 4/5 September 1940. The organization still occupies the site today, making it very easy to replace the modern frontage with its wartime predecessor. The original District Bank building, which once stood a short way to the right of the barracks, has been replaced by the more modern building seen here. The original building can be seen better on the next page.

Damage done during the raid of 4/5 September 1940 to the District Bank (left), on the corner of Marsh Lane and Stanley Road. The bank is no longer standing, however the public house next door is and today is known as The Jollys. It is a rare survivor in this part of Bootle, which has changed so much since the war. In between the two buildings, the side of the Salvation Army Barracks and some of the properties on Stanley Road can just be made out.

Meanwhile in the Crosby area, a series of high explosive bombs fell overnight, but fortunately, they landed mostly in gardens or fields. For the second night in succession, the borough escaped relatively unscathed. Another unusual feature of the bombs which landed on this night was that a large proportion of them were listed as unexploded. It is not clear why this was the case, and such devices could be very dangerous and obstructive to the authorities until they were dealt with. The usual practice was to evacuate people from the surrounding area and to bring in a specialist team to defuse an unexploded bomb. Alternatively, it would sometimes be taken somewhere safer and then detonated. This work was extremely dangerous and the men involved in it were very brave. Without their courage and sacrifice (many lost their lives) the damage done to the region would have been much greater.

Over on the Wirral, bombs landed in Egerton Road in Bebington and Dacre Hill, Rock Lane East and Procter Road in Birkenhead. Low calibre high explosive and incendiary bombs rained down on Wallasey, mostly hitting the Seacombe area. Roads hit included Palermo Street, Kelvin Road, Dock Road and Gorsey Lane. The Cheshire Lines goods yard was also struck. Three parachute mines were also recorded as falling on Heswall, although no damage was reported.

5/6 SEPTEMBER 1940

In Liverpool, bombs hammered the area around Claudia Street in Walton, as well as the St James' Road and Washington Street areas near the Anglican Cathedral (Scott's still unfinished masterpiece had several stained glass windows shattered). The railway system was also affected, with bombs hitting the cutting near Lime Street Station, causing problems on lines running in and out of the station. Falling masonry also blocked the line at Spellow station.

Bootle escaped without serious damage, the only bombs falling either in the fields near the golf course, or near houses in Carrisbrook Road. In Crosby, four people were injured as bombs fell on several locations across the borough, demolishing four houses and doing serious damage to at least six others. Several gas mains were fractured, as was a sewer. These would have made the task of dealing with the damaged houses that much harder. On the Wirral, a small number of oil bombs landed in the dock areas of both Wallasey and Birkenhead but were soon extinguished.

6/7 SEPTEMBER 1940

First came something of a rarity, a daytime raid, mainly focused on Liverpool. There was also a raid on the city that night. The bombs fell on a warehouse in Norfolk Street, and Milners safe works in Smithdown Lane. There, fourteen ARP ambulances were damaged, hindering the city's efforts to help casualties in the bombing raids.

The Anglican Cathedral was once again hit, although it fortunately survived without any major damage for a second night running. During the last few raids, it had lost most of the stained glass in its south facing windows, and had the doors of the children's porch blown in.

In Birkenhead, a children's home known as Kielberg in the Noctorum area was hit. The Gorsey Hey area of Bebington was struck by bombs, while high explosives demolished three houses in New Ferry, killing two and injuring more than thirty people.

8/9 SEPTEMBER 1940

In what was probably yet another attack by a lone raider, bombs fell on Eldon Street and Market Street in Birkenhead. Nobody was killed in either location.

10/11 SEPTEMBER 1940

This raid lasted around three hours, during which time three unexploded bombs landed near an anti-aircraft site in Deysbrook Lane, Liverpool. Houses in Speke Road were also badly damaged, and bombs also fell in the Woolton and West Derby areas of the city.

Damage done to the Anglican Cathedral and nearby streets. The exact date of the wartime photograph used here is unknown, but it was probably taken during the September raids since the king and queen visited the area to see the damage for themselves in November 1940. They stood not far away from where these modern day cars are parked.

On this night, bombs also came down in the Moreton area,, hitting Upton Road and Kingsmead Road, whilst several landed near the River Birket and the railway.

11/12 SEPTEMBER 1940

In Liverpool, an oil bomb and a high explosive did slight damage to a house and telephone wires in Belle Vale Road, Gateacre.

12/13 SEPTEMBER 1940

The first major raid for several days saw an increase in the scale of the damage and casualties. Buildings in the Langton Dock were struck by high explosives, although the police reports did not go into detail about the damage caused. Two other incidents were recorded in more detail however, with houses in Carnatic Road listed as 'extensively damaged by IB'. As this is a reference to incendiaries, it is most likely a case of the houses being burnt out rather than demolished.

The police reports also stated that two houses on Wellington Street, Wavertree were demolished and three people were killed at number 52. High explosive and incendiary bombs also landed on Bebington and Neston doing slight damage to houses in each area.

14/15 SEPTEMBER 1940

The docks in Bootle came under attack, although the damage probably wasn't too serious as the Mersey Docks and Harbour Board's own ARP service was able to deal with the fallout. Crosby saw slightly more damage, with the authorities listing five high explosives and at least eight incendiaries landing across the borough. One person was reported as killed and eight injured.

15/16 SEPTEMBER 1940

On this night, there was a heavy raid over North Liverpool, with Norris Green, Walton, Anfield and Fairfield hit. Some bombs also fell on the airport at Speke. A delayed action bomb exploded at noon the next day, killing an RAF officer and two other ranks who were presumably working to defuse it at the time. The Ice Rink in Prescot Road was hit once more, adding to the damage done earlier in the month.

In Bootle, bombs fell on the Orrell Housing Estate area, particularly around Bailey Drive and Park Lane. Flats in the Green Lane area of Tranmere were also struck by high explosive bombs. As luck would have it, although the damage was serious, nobody was killed. Nearby three high explosives hit the Cammell Laird Shipyards, damaging some of the sheds. The parade ground of a new police station in Bromborough was hit, damaging the buildings and two nearby cars.

16/17 SEPTEMBER 1940

In Liverpool, high explosives damaged buildings on Great Homer Street (where an auxiliary fireman was killed), while incendiaries fell on the Carlton Cinema in Moss Lane. Bootle suffered once more, with two main areas coming under attack. Amongst the roads hit were St John's Road, Brasenose Road, Bedford Place, Annie Road, Menai Road and Springwell Road.

17/18 SEPTEMBER 1940

During a daylight raid, bombs were dropped near the Rootes Aircraft Factory in Speke, and some nearby houses were also damaged. Not done with the city yet, the raiders returned that

The serious damage done to the Central Hydraulic Tower in the Birkenhead docks contrasts starkly with the modern sign in this image. Although the original photo is undated, one possibility is that the tower was hit during the mid September raids.

night inflicting what the police reports described as the 'heaviest casualties to date', which resulted in widespread destruction to shops and houses, in the Knotty Ash, Wavertree and West Derby areas.

One particularly horrific incident was when a series of bombs landed on Stevenson Street in Wavertree. Eight people lost their lives, two whilst sheltering in their homes and six in a street shelter, including a two-year-old and a second child who was only 20-months-old. Eight auxiliary firemen were killed by the same bomb in Green Lane. By the following evening, reports put the casualties at forty-three dead, forty-three seriously injured and 119 slightly injured.

Across the Mersey, in Birkenhead, the residents suffered just as badly, with a large number of streets in the town centre and Tranmere hit by high explosives. Several areas in the dock estate were also hit including Morpeth Dock and the East Float. Some bombs also fell in the Eastham area.

18/19 SEPTEMBER 1940

It was Liverpool which really felt the full force of this night's raid, with damage done to a nurses' home in Fazakerley and railway lines at Brownlow Street and St Michael's station. Walton Prison was also struck, with a bomb scoring a direct hit on K wing. In Aintree, high explosives did little damage to houses, but damaged the British Enka Artificial Silk works, killing one person.

Bootle came under attack again, with the Orrell Housing Estate targeted once more. Amongst the roads hit were Gronow Place, Marmion Avenue and Forbes Place. Also struck were a timber storage yard near to Ford Station and the premises of the Penpoll works (a tin smelting factory), which were hit by incendiaries.

In Crosby, half a dozen high explosives, several incendiaries and at least one oil bomb fell on the borough, injuring seven people, destroying two houses and badly damaging another four. Amongst the roads hit were Manor Avenue, Musker Street, Stirling Avenue, Manor Road Wylva Avenue and De Villiers Avenue.

19/20 SEPTEMBER 1940

In Liverpool, the worst affected areas were Walton, West Derby and Anfield. Two roads in particular saw heavy damage – Rossmore Gardens and Hilary Road, both of which are in the Anfield area. The site of an anti-aircraft battery also had to be abandoned due to an unexploded bomb.

Four high explosives landed in Bootle, but thankfully no houses were hit. Instead they landed on the premises of Williams, Harvey and Co on Altcar Road, a canal bank near Linacre Bridge, a railway cutting near the junction of Marsh Lane and Hawthorne Road and a pavement near St Monica's School on Fernhill Road. In Crosby, several incendiary bombs were scattered across the borough, causing at least five separate incidents.

21/22 SEPTEMBER 1940

In Liverpool, the famous department store of T J Hughes on London Road was hit by high explosives, killing three people in the immediate vicinity. Another five people died elsewhere on London Road.

A number of the victims were Air Raid Precaution (ARP) Wardens, and this was probably due to the fact that there was a ARP post on London Road. Elsewhere in the city, two bombs

Damage to the side of the Queens public house on Gray Street, Bootle done during the night of 21/22 September 1940.

Above: Damage done to the property on the corner of Bedford Road and Cambridge Road, Bootle. The photograph is undated, but these buildings were probably hit during the night of 21/22 September 1940, when both roads are recorded as being struck. The corner building has since been replaced with post war garages. This view looks along Bedford Road. This road was hit several times during the air raids, including one incident during the May Blitz when the Bedford Road School had its roof severely damaged by fires that were started by incendiary bombs.

Left: The contents of this wartime cotton warehouse cascade onto the modern day Nelson Street. It was definitely hit on the night of 21/22 September 1940.

penetrated the Mersey Underground Railway and badly damaged two trains. Other bombs forced the closure of sections of the East Lancs Road and London Road. No less than eighteen unexploded bombs were reported across the city.

In Bootle, hundreds of small incendiary bombs fell mainly along the lengths of Derby and Rimrose Road. As both of these were within a stone's throw of the docks, there were less people around to put the flames out before the fires took hold, and before long, many timber yards and warehouses were soon burning fiercely. Nearly two dozen high explosives were scattered across the borough, demolishing ten houses and seriously damaging a further eighty-nine. Twenty-one people died and around sixty were injured.

In Crosby, two high explosives landed on the borough at just past midnight on 22 September, one on 30 Rothesay Drive and the other on 36 Caithness Drive. Nobody was killed at either location, but five people were injured.

Amongst the roads hit in Wallasey were Lily Grove, Briardale Road, Alfred Road, and Hawthorne Grove. Some of the bombs had a delayed action fuse, which caused great problems. Sadly five people were killed during the attack on the borough.

In Birkenhead, the Argyle Theatre had to be closed after it received damage from a bomb that hit Argyle Street.

23/24 SEPTEMBER 1940
The raiders attacking Liverpool concentrated mostly on the northern part of the city, hitting mostly residential areas. Two areas mentioned specifically by the police reports were Robson Street and the chapel in Walton Park Cemetery.

In Bootle, the high explosive bombs that fell were concentrated around an anti-aircraft gun site that was positioned on the Municipal Golf Course. Fortunately, this only resulted in several large craters being left in the grass as none of the explosives struck the vital guns. Incendiaries were also dropped on the Orrell area, especially around Springwell Road, Park Lane and Bailey Drive.

In Crosby, ten high explosive bombs and many more incendiaries struck the town. Somehow there were no casualties, although three buildings were listed as being badly damaged.

24/25 SEPTEMBER 1940
The night saw a continuation of the heavy attacks on Liverpool. Amongst the targets hit were a cotton warehouse on Clegg Street, the Stanley Tobacco Warehouse, the premises of Silcocks on Great Howard Street, and the Love Lane area. Shops in the city centre were also struck, specifically in Church Street, Clayton Square and Parker Street.

25/26 SEPTEMBER 1940
Raiders dropped bombs on the Crosby area, all of which landed at around 10.00 pm. A single high explosive hit Somerset Road, whilst around a dozen fell harmlessly on the Waterloo shore, in the area opposite Adelaide Terrace and Beach Lane. Three people were injured and a small number of buildings suffered minor damage.

26/27 SEPTEMBER 1940
Liverpool suffered badly during the night's raid, with extensive damage done to Wapping, Queens, Kings, Coburg and Brunswick Docks. Thirteen warehouses were seriously damaged along with their contents. The Admiralty Stores in Canning Place were demolished, and a

high explosive bomb landed between the Port of Liverpool Building and Cunard Building on Brunswick Street, doing slight damage to each.

In Birkenhead, the famous Argyle Theatre was struck by incendiary bombs. The resulting fire destroyed the interior of the building, leaving the stage and auditorium ruined. Other areas hit in the borough included Beckwith Street, Carlisle Street, Eldon Street, Livingstone Street and the London Midland Scottish and Great Western Railway marshalling yards. Part of the roof of the tunnel between Birkenhead Park station and Hamilton Square station collapsed after damage from the bombs, blocking the line.

In Wallasey, around a hundred magnesium bombs (a type of incendiary bomb) landed on the borough, damaging properties in Edgmond Street, Kelvin Road and Borough Road. There were no casualties and most of the bombs were dealt with before the fires could become serious.

In Bebington, bombs landed in Kirkway, off Higher Bebington Road.

27/28 SEPTEMBER 1940
Bombs fell on houses in Great Homer Street, Liverpool, demolishing some of them. A school in Banks Road, Garston was also hit by a high explosive bomb, doing some damage.

28/29 SEPTEMBER 1940
A raid concentrated solely on Birkenhead, saw bombs falling on Carlisle Street, Grange Road, Mather Road and Slatey Road. One of the principal buildings struck that night was the police station which once stood at the corner of Slatey Road and Mather Road, next to the Williamson Art Gallery.

Damage to Slatey Road Police Station in Birkenhead done on the night of 28/29 September 1940. No longer still standing, its exact scale and position was worked out from maps and old photographs. The building on the right is the Williamson Art Gallery. Given that at least two devices landed in close proximity to the gallery, Birkenhead can consider itself fortunate that it survived the raids without any significant damage.

The view down Mather Road, Birkenhead from near its junction with Slatey Road. The damage seen here was done during the same raid as the photograph above, most likely from another high explosive bomb. The archives list numbers 32-38 as suffering the worst damage. According to the civilian roll of honour, nobody was killed in either road that night.

29/30 SEPTEMBER 1940

Liverpool was hit again, although most of the devices dropped were incendiary bombs which landed on the Everton and Aigburth districts. Fires were started at the Hamlet Free Church in Aigburth and at a nearby laundry, but were soon extinguished. In addition, some of the bombs caused serious damage to oil cake, flax and grain warehouses in the Dukes Dock area. A collapsing wall also killed two auxiliary firemen.

A series of large calibre high explosive bombs landed in several locations in the Wallasey area. Amongst the places hit were Buckingham Road, Southcroft Road, Falkland Road, Rudgrave Square, Wright Street, Wallacre Park, the Hillside Road allotments and Paul's recreation ground. Bombs also set fire to the LMS warehouse in Egerton Dock, as well as storage facilities in Grange Road, Birkenhead, but were soon brought under control.

30 SEPTEMBER/1 OCTOBER 1940

In Birkenhead, incendiaries fell on Balls Road, Carlisle Street, Chester Street and Kingsland Road. In Bidston, the Wirral Ladies' Golf Club was hit. Meanwhile in New Ferry some properties in Rock Park were struck by the bombs.

1/2 OCTOBER 1940

In Liverpool, the only devices dropped were some incendiary bombs scattered over East Toxteth Dock.

Birkenhead was less fortunate, with both incendiaries and high explosives striking a number of sites across the town. One feature of the damage was shattered gas mains, which caused huge problems for the rescue workers. At one point, gas masks had to be used to prevent the fumes from overcoming the workers.

7/8 OCTOBER 1940

A raid on Liverpool lasted nearly four hours, and left significant damage. High explosive bombs landed in the area of Great Mersey Street and Stanley Road, whilst others came down on Lichfield Road and Grantley Road in Wavertree. Most of the damage was residential, but a Welsh Chapel on Great Mersey street was also demolished by one of the bombs.

8/9 OCTOBER 1940

A Junkers JU88 bomber was brought to earth near Bromborough Dock shortly after 4.00 pm, shot down by a combination of anti-aircraft fire and the attacks of three fighter pilots based in Speke. Of the four man crew, three survived, although one was badly injured. They were captured by Harry Gill, a gateman at Bromborough Dock who disarmed them despite being alone and unarmed.

Later that evening a lone raider dropped bombs on the Woodchurch Road area of Birkenhead.

10/11 OCTOBER 1940

The attack on Liverpool came in two waves. The first was focused on Everton Valley, Knotty Ash, Mossley Hill and Mill Street, whilst the second was mainly concentrated on the Anfield area. Two incidents mentioned specifically were at Manningham Road and Hogarth Road.

Bootle also came under attack, and a number of incendiary bombs were scattered across the town, but the damage was confined to houses in Chesnut Grove and St Paul's Church in Balfour Road. On the Wirral, incendiaries fell near Eastham Locks, whilst high explosives fell on the Unilever Works in Port Sunlight, and also on some homes in Bromborough Pool village.

11/12 OCTOBER 1940

Once again, the raiders attacked Liverpool in two distinct waves. They first attacked the city centre and North Docks areas, severely damaging South John Street, James Street, Redcross Street, Paradise Street, Hanover Street and South Castle Street. The second raid struck at the areas around Hill Street and Bankhall Street, doing damage to the Admiralty stores and nearby railway lines. A bomb struck the Cunard Building, but fortunately failed to explode. Alexandra and Langton Dock were also hit.

A total of ten bombs landed in the Regent Road area of Bootle. Prominent targets included the Summer Seat Timber Yard, Alexandra Dock Passenger Station, Alexandra Dock Goods Station, a grain warehouse and the Boys' Secondary School on Balliol Road. The bombs fractured water mains and telephone cables in several places.

Balliol Road School, Bootle struck by high explosive bombs during the raid on the night of 11/12 October 1940. This photograph also acts as a correction to my second book, which placed the building on the far side of Balliol Road. The school would be struck again later in the raids and for a time, classes were relocated to houses on the other side of Balliol Road. The building has been replaced by modern college buildings.

The school was perhaps the worst affected, with one bomb penetrating to the ground floor of the building on the south eastern corner. That side of the building was badly damaged too, whilst the tower was also affected. Another bomb landed nearby in College View. Eight people were injured by the bombs and there was one fatality.

Crosby experienced more than a dozen separate incidents involving incendiary bombs. Two people were injured but the damage to buildings was very slight, especially when compared to the destruction to the south.

Wallasey came under attack once more, with electron magnesium bombs falling on Wheatland Lane. An incendiary bomb also fell on the Great Float Hotel, landing on a billiard table. The owner's luck held though, as it burnt itself out without doing any serious damage. A bomb also fell at the junction of Brimstage Road and Clatterbridge Road on the Wirral, blocking both.

13/14 OCTOBER 1940

Raiders struck at Liverpool, with some bombs falling on Gladstone and North Hornby Dock, whilst others landed on the Myrtle Gardens tenements. Eleven people were reported killed at the latter, and nine were injured. Properties on Gadsby Street and Lime Street were also badly damaged.

Birkenhead was hit particularly hard that night, with the town centre, Prenton and Lower Tranmere areas hammered by both high explosive and incendiary bombs.

The ground floor of the former Boilermaker's Hall on Argyle Street showing the kind of damage that would make it tricky to sell if it was still present on its modern day replacement.

Damage done to numbers 1 and 3 Bedford Road, Wallasey, seen after the raid on 13/14 October 1940. The trees in the background are in part of the Rake Lane cemetery.

View of the serious damage done to numbers 87 and 89 Withens Lane, Wallasey, during the night raid on 13/14 October 1940. Fortunately nobody was killed.

One of the night's probable victims was the Boilermaker's Hall on Argyle Street in Birkenhead. Although not specifically mentioned in most reports, it did stand very close to the Savoy Cinema, and a bomb is recorded as having fallen nearby. Three people were killed in one incident in Henry Street.

In Wallasey, bombs fell on Withens Lane, Linden Grove, Kirk Cottages, Longland Road, Bedford Road, Wallasey Golf Links, Harrison Drive, some gun emplacements near the Promenade and St Mary's Church.

16/17 OCTOBER 1940

In Liverpool, incendiaries fell on the Walton and Everton districts, whilst a surface shelter in Louisa Street was hit by a high explosive bomb, killing eight and injuring more than twenty people. Other roads hit included Breckfield Road, Venmore Street, Pagewood Street, Brandon Street, Beacon Lane and St George's Church, Everton.

Birkenhead was once again targeted by the Luftwaffe. Incendiary bombs fell between Upton and Bidston station. Bombs also rained down on Mersey Park and on the Quigeley Flats in Tranmere.

17/18 OCTOBER 1940

The west wing of Fazakerley Sanatorium was demolished, killing a soldier who was a patient there. High Explosives also damaged houses in West Derby, as well as striking a school, whilst incendiaries fell on the Lark Lane and Ullet Road areas. A delayed action bomb landed in the yard of Morrison School, causing evacuation of the vicinity.

Numbers 18 and 20 Patrick Avenue, Bootle. Furniture on the street was a common sight after raids, as the bombed-out residents attempted to salvage whatever they could. Although the photograph is undated, there was only one occasion during the blitz on which the road received damage – the night of 17/18 October 1940. The archive mentions four houses being demolished in the avenue on that night and others damaged, but only this photograph appears to have been taken at the time.

At least three serious incidents occurred in Bootle. An unexploded bomb was reported to the rear of houses on Southport Road, but before it could be defused it exploded, demolishing three houses and damaging others.

Another unexploded bomb buried itself in Park Lane, but this one was defused and safely removed by the bomb squad. In Patrick Avenue, four houses were demolished and many more were badly damaged.

Meanwhile, Crosby was victim to a most unusual type of damage – friendly fire. In this case, the culprit was falling anti-aircraft shells. One fell on number 41 York Avenue, whilst another struck a house called Dalmore on Merrilocks Road.

In the Birkenhead area, a mix of incendiaries and high explosives fell in several areas. Upton Road in Bidston was hit, whilst an unexploded bomb was reported outside the Aerowata works in Russell Road, Rock Ferry, which exploded four hours after landing. In Tranmere, bombs fell on Hawthorne Road, Well Lane and New Chester Road, landing on the Cammell Laird Shipyards and the Thompson Glue Works.

In New Ferry, bombs landed on Boundary Road, while in Port Sunlight three people died when a bomb struck 55 Pool Bank.

18/19 OCTOBER 1940

In a raid that lasted around three hours, bombers brought destruction to houses in the Norris Green area of the city. Some areas in South Liverpool were also hit and police reports describe St Clement's Church on Beaumont Street in Toxteth as being 'seriously damaged'.

19/20 OCTOBER 1940

Raiders continued to pound Liverpool in a raid that lasted nearly five hours. Houses and shops on High Park Street in Toxteth were hit, as was the Seamen's Orphanage in Tuebrook. The high explosive bomb which struck the latter did some damage, but fortunately. failed to explode. St Silas' Church which stood on Pembroke Place was also struck.

Wallasey saw several large bombs land on the borough. They struck Belgrave Street, Coningsby Drive, Merton Road, Tancred Road, Hazeldene Avenue and Wallasey Road.

One wing of a trench shelter in the Belvidere Recreation Ground was also hit. By a stroke of good fortune, it had been waterlogged for some time, which meant it was empty at the time of the raid. Elsewhere though, two people were killed in the raid and two were injured.

21/22 OCTOBER 1940

At around 7.30 am on 21 October 1940, a raider dropped high explosive bombs near the Rootes Aircraft Factory in Speke. Slight damage was done to overhead electric wires, but otherwise the factory escaped without harm. Later that night, Liverpool was again targeted. Houses were damaged on Dacy Road, two tramcars were hit on Priory Road and in the Aigburth Road area service mains were damaged and both sides of the road were blocked. Incendiaries also landed on Speke, West Derby, Croxteth and Huyton.

In Bootle, the raid was concentrated primarily on a north-south line along Stanley Road, with the area being battered by six high explosive bombs. The first fell opposite the Imperial Cinema. The second completely demolished a food warehouse called Costigans. The next two caused damage in Oregon Street, Virginia Street and Garfield Street where a street shelter was hit.

The Imperial Cinema, Bootle showing the scars of the late October raids. The building was hit during the night of 21/22 October 1940.

The final two landed in Crete Street and Malta Road. A separate bomb fell on Forshaw's timber yard in Marsh Lane. A total of seven people were killed in the raid, eight were seriously injured and eight lightly injured. Ten houses were demolished in the borough and more than 160 were slightly damaged.

The raiders also struck at Borrowdale Road and the Gorsey Hey area of Higher Bebington, whilst two high explosive bombs also badly damaged houses in Lower Bebington. Around sixty incendiaries landed on the foreshore at Hoylake, near Hilbre Island.

25/26 OCTOBER 1940

In Liverpool, bombs fell on Richmond Park, demolishing three houses and doing serious damage to Holy Trinity School. A slight fire was also started at the Mill Lane Rope Works. In Bootle, there was a short raid, during which bombs fell on Alexandra Dock Railway Yard and an adjoining timber yard. They damaged railway wagons, a railway siding and a stock of hard wood timber.

Meanwhile more than half a dozen different places in Crosby were hit by incendiary bombs, but very little damage was done.

26/27 OCTOBER 1940

The night's raid took a grim toll on the people living near the Netherfield Road area of Liverpool. Heavy calibre high explosive bombs shattered at least three buildings on the road and seriously damaged another thirty. Four public houses were also badly damaged.

An ARP post was demolished, killing one warden and injuring another. Around sixteen people were trapped in damaged buildings, and despite the best efforts of the surviving wardens at least eleven people lost their lives.

In Crosby, incendiary bombs rained onto the borough once more. This time they fell almost entirely on the foreshore at Seaforth, although a single high explosive also landed near Beach Lawn.

27/28 OCTOBER 1940

The raiders returned for another night with bombs falling mostly on the Dock Estate. A serious fire was started in a shed in the Queens Dock area, but was soon brought under control. Sadly, three crew members at the nearby AFS post were killed by the bombs. A pub on Bridgewater Street was damaged, whilst high explosives landed on Falkner Street, Branstree Avenue, Scargreen Avenue and Chaloner Street.

In Bootle, another eight hour raid saw incendiaries fall over a wide area, providing an aiming mark for other planes. High explosives soon followed, demolishing a wing of St John's School and four houses in Brasenose Road. Another bomb landed at the junction of St John's Road and Bedford Place, demolishing a similar number of houses. A third struck a railway tunnel in St John's Road. The total damage in Bootle was nine houses demolished, twenty seriously damaged and 116 slightly damaged. Nine people were injured and two were killed.

On the Wirral, bombs fell on Bebington, where they damaged ten houses and the soap works of Unilever. Also hit was a delivery company's premises in Bromborough, two wooden bungalows in Irby, and properties at the corner of Upton Road and Noctorum Avenue in Birkenhead.

St John's School, in Brasenose Road, Bootle. Both the school and the church it was connected to have long since gone, leaving behind no trace and making a comparison such as this one particularly challenging. Most of the area is now taken up with commercial premises. The school was a victim of the raid on the night of 27/28 October 1940. The Church would have stood on the far left of this photograph.

29 OCTOBER 1940

After two air raid warnings nothing happened, but then bombs began to land at 8.00 pm. The telephone exchange in South John Street was hit and temporarily put out of action. Business premises in South Castle Street were also superficially damaged. The School of Domestic Science on Wood Street was set alight, but was soon made safe again.

Several places on Bold Street in the city centre were hit by incendiary bombs, as was a railway siding in Speke, and also the Matchworks building in Garston. None of these hits resulted in fires, though. Queens Dock was also hit, as was Thomas Street where two warehouses were demolished. Meanwhile, a single high explosive bomb landed in Gayton on the Wirral but did little damage.

1/2 NOVEMBER 1940

In Liverpool, the raiders scattered incendiary bombs on the County Road, Great Howard Street and the East Lancs Road. Melia's Food Distributors on Love Lane was hit, as was Gwladys Street School and Arnot Street School. The small fires these bombs started caused some slight damage.

In Bootle, the raid was comparatively short, with relatively minor damage done. High explosive bombs landed on Peel Road, Bulwer Street, Goldsmith Street and Burns Street. Light damage was done to thirty-seven houses, whilst eight were badly damaged. Fortunately though, only two people were injured. In Crosby, high explosives landed on Kendrick Street, Arthur Street and Verdi Street. Also hit was a timber yard on Lathom Avenue, a first aid post in Rawson Road, the greyhound racing track, and the garden at the rear of the Merchant Taylors' Old Boys' Club.

Grosvenor Road, Wallasey, hit during the early November raids. Originally the premises of a laundry firm, the building would be seriously damaged in a later raid, with around half of it being lost. This particular photo was taken after the raid on the night of 1/2 November 1940.

Three incendiary bombs also landed on a tip and waste ground in Ronald Road, whilst an anti-aircraft shell crashed to earth at 15 Elton Avenue. Two people were injured in this raid, one building was completely destroyed, and four more were badly damaged.

In Wallasey, the raid took place during a very heavy thunderstorm, with the raiders concentrating mostly on the New Brighton area. Many barrage balloons were struck by lightning and were brought crashing to earth. Bombs struck Rowson Street, Grosvenor Road, Cressingham Road, Dalmorton Road, Tollemache Street, Vyner Road, Albert Street and Victoria Road. The total casualties were five dead and three wounded.

2/3 NOVEMBER 1940
A number of incendiary bombs were scattered across the Gorsey Hey area of Bebington, doing relatively little damage.

4/5 NOVEMBER 1940
On this particular night, there were three separate alert periods for Liverpool. During the first one, high explosive bombs landed on Townsend Avenue and the Wavertree Playground areas. Two houses were seriously damaged and a further fifteen slightly damaged. A gas main was also fractured and caught fire, but by a stroke of luck, the fire was put out by water flowing from a nearby burst water main. Sandyville Road and Garfield Road in Clubmoor were also hit. The second and third alerts were without incident.

5 NOVEMBER 1940
The king and queen visited Wallasey during the day to see for themselves the dreadful damage that had been inflicted on the area. Large crowds cheered them wherever they went. They spoke to families affected by the raids and various dignitaries and members of the civil defence units.

The king and queen pass along Littledale Road, Wallasey.

6 NOVEMBER 1940
Following their visit to Wallasey, the king and queen went on to Birkenhead. They arrived at Woodside Station, and then visited the Town Hall, Market Street, Chester Street and Union Street.

8/9 NOVEMBER 1940
This was a brief raid with only a few incendiaries landing in the Childwall Valley Road area.

12/13 NOVEMBER 1940
In a night raid which lasted just over an hour, several bombs landed on the Liverpool. Four high explosives landed within half a mile of the Edge Hill Railway Goods Station, demolishing three houses and damaging others nearby. An incendiary also landed on the roof of the Post Office in Wavertree Road causing slight damage to it. One of the sites hit by the raiders was Sidney Place, where ten people died and three houses were demolished. In Saxony Road, a further three people were killed when a surface shelter was hit. Edinburgh Road was also hit and several houses were damaged, but nobody died.

Birkenhead saw two high explosives fall in the Vyner Road area, two more in Noctorum Village and an oil bomb land in Duke Street. In Wallasey, high calibre explosives landed in the dock area, including the Cheshire Goods Yard and Gorsey Lane Gas Works. Bombs also fell on Claughton Drive, Poulton Road and Mill Lane Yard. Nine people were slightly injured across the borough.

17/18 NOVEMBER 1940

Incendiary bombs were dropped on Liverpool. A house on Guest Street was hit during the night, as was a warehouse in Sefton Street. No casualties were reported. A number of barrage balloons were reported as falling from the skies in flames, which was put down to atmospheric conditions rather than enemy action.

18/19 NOVEMBER 1940

This raid lasted around three hours, with the Anfield and Aigburth areas of Liverpool hit. A large number of incendiaries fell on both of those places, with some high explosives mixed in doing more damage. Many of the devices dropped had an explosive element, making them much more dangerous than those previously used, and about ten people were injured trying to deal with them.

In Aigburth, two houses were demolished in Wingate Road, where five people died, whilst high explosives also fell on Aigburth Vale High School, St Anne's School, Elmar Road, Braunton Road and Latrigg Road. In Anfield, three houses were demolished in Teulon Street and three people died. Priory Road, Hornsey Road and Watford Road were also hit, with one person being killed at the latter. Incendiary bombs also landed in the grounds of Liverpool College and on Christ Church in Linnet Lane.

In Bromborough, incendiaries landed near the central power station but did no damage, whilst in Eastham, they fell on fields, but merely set some haystacks alight. Half a dozen bombs also exploded on the foreshore near Meols.

20/21 NOVEMBER 1940

Birkenhead town centre came under attack again, with bombs falling on Carlisle Street and Westbourne Road. In Prenton, they fell in fields and on the Golf Links.

22/23 NOVEMBER 1940

The overnight raid on Liverpool was fairly short, lasting just twenty-four minutes. High explosive bombs landed in the Great Homer Street area, damaging houses and shops. In Wallasey, a single bomb fell at the rear of the Swan Hotel on the Dock Road but did very little damage.

23/24 NOVEMBER 1940

A stick of bombs fell on Fielden Road, Birkenhead whilst another eight landed in Lower Bebington, demolishing one house and doing slight damage to another ten.

28/29 NOVEMBER 1940

After a short lull, the Luftwaffe returned with full force, causing extensive damage across almost the entire region overnight. It was Liverpool though that was hit the worst, with even the police reports recording it as the 'heaviest raid to date'. No less than thirty parachute mines were scattered across the city, although eight of them failed to explode. The raid began with incendiary bombs, then proceeded onto high explosives and parachute mines in short order.

A bomb shattered 38 Rose Place (off Scotland Road), killing no less than eight members of the Armstrong family and damaging the nearby St Anne's Church. Three more people were killed when 69 Granby Street was struck. In Wavertree, a road called Ashfield was hammered and sixteen people lost their lives.

In Spofforth Road, the raiders claimed the lives of another nine people and also damaged the nearby gas works. Considerable damage was done to the Holland Street and Ardleigh Road districts, whilst incendiaries were scattered across Allerton, Wavertree and Childwall. A shelter in the Botanic Gardens was hit, killing two people. Some of those bombed out of the shelter are thought to have sought safety in the ill-fated Durning Road shelter.

Other spots struck that night included the Picton Road Gasworks, St Thomas' Church in Anfield, Greenheys Road, Rose Hill Police Station, St Joseph's School in Grosevenor Street, the Adelphi Cinema in Christian Street and North Gladstone Dock. Parachute mines also badly damaged Heygreen Road and the junction of Fernwood Road and Birch Tree Road in Aigburth, where, tragically, twenty-six people were killed.

Olive Mount Children's Hospital, St Mary's Church, Sandown Park, Webster Road Council Schools, Liverpool College, Aigburth Cricket Ground and Bishop's Lodge were also damaged by parachute mines. Bombs also started serious fires on a shed in Garston Docks, the Highfield Sanatorium and the Picton Road Gasworks.

The biggest incident of the night and indeed of the entire war for Merseyside, occurred in the Edge Hill area of Liverpool at the Ernest Brown Junior Instructional Centre on Durning Road (it is generally known as the 'Durning Road Incident'). Here, more than 300 people were packed into a basement shelter, but at around 2.00 am, a parachute mine collapsed the building above, with debris cascading down into the basement and burying alive many of those present. Part of the basement included a boiler room, and the boiler now burst, filling the shelter with hot water. To add to this hellish scene, a nearby gas pipe burst and caught fire. The survivors would somehow have to negotiate these horrific obstacles to escape the shelter. Even with the heroic efforts of rescue workers and locals, an estimated 180 people were still killed, and only 30 people escaped without injury. Prime Minister Winston Churchill described it as 'the worst single civilian incident of the whole war'.

Meanwhile, the people of Bootle were introduced to a terrifying new weapon they had not seen used before – the parachute mine. These were much larger and more powerful than the average German high explosive bomb, and caused virtually all of the major single incidents associated with heavy loss of life during the blitz.

Three went off in the borough that night at the following locations: The canal goods warehouse on Carolina Street, causing extensive damage, and demolishing (or damaging so badly that they were beyond hope of repair) nine houses in the street. Concord Place was virtually wiped out with fifteen houses damaged there, while ten houses were hit in Boston Street.

In addition, the corner of Trinity Road and University Road, where the Presbyterian Chapel stood, were partly demolished. Five large houses were destroyed, whilst another fifteen nearby were badly damaged. Water, gas and electric mains supplies to the area were fractured. An insulating factory on Hawthorne Road was also hit, causing serious damage to the premises and the adjoining businesses, and slightly damaging some of the houses nearby.

A fourth, unexploded mine landed on the railway embankment, close to the junction of Aintree Road and Hawthorne Road. A total of six people were killed, four badly injured and thirty-six slightly injured.

In Crosby, high explosive bombs landed right across the borough, accompanied by separate incidents involving incendiaries. The high explosives landed on the foreshore near Harbord Road, the rear garden of 17 Old Farm Road, Muspratt's Field and two in the grounds

Bootle Protestant Free Church, which stood not far from the location where the second parachute mine exploded on 28/29 November 1940. The road on the right is University Road, and the one in the foreground is Trinity Road. Several men are standing near the corner of the two roads, with one of them appearing to carry a long handled brush. A modern church stands on the site now having opened in 1948.

of Little Crosby Hall. The incendiaries landed mostly in fields, although some landed in Newborough Avenue. Two people were injured in the raid, but fortunately there were no fatalities.

Birkenhead was hammered by bombs, which fell on Arkle Road, Lansdowne Place, Norman Street, Browning Avenue, Egerton Park, Henry Street and Clifton Road. In Bebington, bombs landed in Heyville Road and Sumner Street. Thornton Hough, Gayton, Barnston, Neston and New Ferry were also hit.

Despite the extensive damage to the rest of the region, Wallasey appears to have survived this dreadful night unscathed. Reports made five days after the raid give the casualties for Liverpool alone at 264 dead, sixty-two seriously injured, and 253 slightly injured.

29/30 NOVEMBER 1940

After the horrors of the previous night, the people of Merseyside were no doubt relieved that this raid was a relatively minor one. It lasted just over an hour, with damage confined to houses in Church Road, Robson Street and Tapley Place in Liverpool. Incendiaries also fell on Belmont Road Hospital but no serious damage was done.

THE CHRISTMAS BLITZ, DECEMBER 1940

After the horrific raids towards the end of November 1940, the first few weeks of December were relatively peaceful with only scattered attacks to keep the civil defences on their toes and the people alert to danger. The Bootle authorities noted that the air raid sirens went off fourteen times in the first three weeks of the month, making it difficult for people to sleep properly.

This period of calm was not to last though, and beginning on the night of 20 December and continuing for three nights, the Luftwaffe pounded the region mercilessly, paying no heed to the fact that the season of goodwill was just around the corner. Although outside the scope of this book, it is worth noting that Manchester was also heavily bombed on the nights of 22/23 and 23/24 December, with nearly 700 people killed and over 2,000 wounded.

For most of the region, this three-night nightmare was the second worst period of the entire blitz in terms of casualties and damage done. Wallasey, for example, had five times as many casualties in the Christmas Blitz as it had suffered in the entire bombardment up until that point. Coming in such a short space of time, and on the back of the heavy raids at the end of November 1940, it must have seemed like a particularly dark period for those that lived through the events.

Numbers 12 and 14 Greenheys Road, Wallasey showing the heavy damage they received during the Christmas Raids. This is one of many photographs of the period that is undated, other than it being sometime in the final month of 1940.

18 DECEMBER 1940

In what appears to have been an isolated incident, bombs fell on Rockybank Road, Higher Tranmere.

20/21 DECEMBER 1940

The night's raid began just after 6.00 pm and lasted until 4.00 am, highlighting that the enemy was clearly determined to make the best use possible of the long winter nights. In Liverpool, the raids opened with incendiaries, but high explosive bombs and parachute mines were soon added, the latter doing extensive damage where they came down. The North Docks were particularly badly hit, with nine men killed when a parachute mine exploded at Waterloo Dock. Extensive fires were also started there, as many of the goods they contained were flammable such as hardwood, rubber or oil.

Another mine came to earth near the side of the Adelphi Hotel, close to its junction with Bolton Street. In addition to badly damaging that side of the hotel, many of the buildings facing onto Copperas Hill between Bolton Street and Hilbre Street were flattened and several parked cars were thrown up against each other.

A high explosive bomb created a crater in Roe Street, which a fire engine later fell into. St Nicholas' Church near the pierhead was also severely damaged. Incendiaries started fires throughout the city, with several notable buildings being affected, including the Town Hall, the Municipal Buildings and the Cunard Buildings. Incendiaries also fell on both the Lewis's and Blackler's department stores, but the fire watchers on duty at both retailers were able to deal with the few fires they started very efficiently.

Damage done to the Copperas Hill side of the Adelphi Hotel, including broken windows. Note the dented sides of the cars, suggesting that they were thrown against each other by the force of the explosion – in this case from a parachute mine. The same device is thought to have devastated one side of Copperas Hill, between Bolton Street and Hilbre Street.

A bomb fell on the communal shelter by Blackstock Gardens, killing at least seventy people, many of whom had only just got off trams which had been brought to a stop nearby due to the air raid.

In Bootle, the attacks followed a very similar pattern, with incendiaries falling mostly in the area between the docks and Hawthorne Road. If the intention had been to start fires to direct the bombers that followed, this was largely unsuccessful as the blazes started by the incendiaries were minimal.

Damage to numbers 120-136 Benedict Street, Bootle, where six people were killed and many more injured on the night of 20/21 December 1940. The damage was done by a parachute mine which exploded between Benedict Street and Olivia Street.

Also hit on this first night of the Christmas Blitz, were these houses on Kings Road in Bootle. The nearest house was number 64. All of these wartime properties have been demolished since the raids and modern housing, which stand between Keble Road and Exeter Road has taken their place.

Two views of the properties near the junction of Church Street and Church Alley, damaged during the Christmas Blitz. They were effectively destroyed and later pulled down to be replaced by Spinney House. That was built for the Littlewoods firm, but is no longer occupied by it.

Both wartime images seem to have been taken shortly after the raids as civil defence workers are still fighting fires.

The devices which followed caused damage in Keble Road, Queen's Road, Radnor Drive, Brookhill Road, Morningside Road and Kings Road. A heavy bomb fell in Millers Bridge, near the junction with Regent Road. The damage was quite extensive, with a public house, thirty-one houses and warehouses all hit. In Hawthorne Road, bombs demolished numbers 250 and 252, whilst another twenty houses were affected in a separate incident. Numbers 88 and 90 Gloucester Road were badly damaged nearby, as were seven houses in Vaux Crescent.

A high explosive bomb fell in Rimrose Road, near the junction with Lyster Road, damaging the road bridge over a railway line to the docks. The same device also caused damage to the gas, electricity and water mains in the area and ripped up a tram track, putting it out of action.

Parachute mines were once again responsible for some of the worst incidents. One fell between Benedict Street and Olivia Street, destroying thirteen houses and damaging more than thirty. Another fell on Aintree Road, near St Monica's School, damaging nearly sixty nearby houses and the school itself. Berry Street was also hit by a mine, with seven houses

Numbers 74-108 Aintree Road in Bootle, near the junction with Southport Road, were damaged in the raid on 20/21 December 1940. Of particular note is the overturned car near the central reservation, presumably this was caught up in the blast. To the left of the car, is a small lorry and someone pushing a large pram along the pavement. Although every window and door appears to have been blown in, the damage was comparatively slight and all these houses still stand today.

demolished, twenty-nine seriously damaged and seventy slightly. Another deadly mine landed between Bianca and Viola Street, destroying fourteen houses.

A final mine landed in Pembroke Road but failed to explode. A Royal Navy disposal squad was eventually called and was able to make the device safe and remove it. The Royal Navy was employed in this case as the mines were actually designed as naval weapons, intended to sink in water and damage shipping, but they proved to be just as destructive when used on land. The residents were evacuated, and were extremely fortunate to have escaped so lightly.

A single parachute mine could have a devastating impact, as these two photographs show. The roads are parallel to each other and it is believed that just one mine caused all the damage in each road, since no other devices are recorded as falling in the area on the night in question. This first image depicts the remains of numbers 36 and 38 Viola Street. Between the two streets, nearly thirty people were killed.

The houses either side of number 25 Bianca Street Bootle, following the explosion of a parachute mine to the rear of the houses on the night of 20/21 December 1940. The area has changed somewhat since the war, making it difficult to gauge the exact scale of the long demolished wartime properties. In this case, some idea could be gained from the house on the left, which may well be pre-war.

Crosby suffered as well, with high explosives landing on Muspratt's field, on fields near Little Crosby Road and in the grounds of Crosby Hall. A parachute mine landed on 70 Cambridge Road, Waterloo and initially failed to explode, but eventually went off on the 22 December at 2:30 am Incendiaries also came down, landing on Bowersdale Park, Kingsway, Middleton Road and near the Hall Road AFS Station. There were no casualties and comparatively few houses were damaged.

In Wallasey, two major incidents occurred in Withens Lane. In the first of these, three people were killed near the junction with Urmson Road, when a house was demolished and another severely damaged. A bomb also landed on the William Fletcher Rogers Nursing Home, near the junction of Withens Lane and Manor Road. The home specialized in the care of the elderly, and unfortunately, thirteen residents lost their lives, partly due to being trapped in the rubble and partly because a nearby gas mains had broken and was spewing out fumes.

The remains of the William Fletcher Rogers nursing home seen from Withens Lane, Wallasey after the damage done on the night of 20/21 December 1940. Thirteen elderly residents lost their lives despite the best efforts of the wardens. The tower on the left is part of St Mary's Church. The site of the nursing home is now occupied by a small block of modern flats.

A man is about to walk past the wartime damage to Withens Lane and enter the modern world of Urmson Road. The house nearest to him would have been number 61 Withens Lane. Although the two locations on this page are close to each other, it is unlikely that it was the same bomb that caused the damage, since the corner of the nursing home closest to these houses is the one least damaged.

Another incident occurred on Manor Road, near the junction with Belgrave Street. The bombers demolished or badly damaged several houses in this area, including 54 Manor Road where two people were killed. One of them was William Tyers, from Nottingham, who had spent his life at sea, eventually rising to the rank of captain with the Brocklebank Shipping Line. William was nearly 70 at the time of his death. A 38-year-old woman called Elsie Josephine Denvir also died here.

Next door at number 56, four members of the Brayshaw family were killed. Grace Elizabeth, who was 70, and her husband John, 69, were killed alongside their daughters Grace Matilda, 40, and Marjorie, 42.

At number 58, Alexander Ramsey, aged 50, died, as did Janet Potter, who at 80, would have been one of the oldest victims of the air raids.

Manor Road from the junction with Belgrave Street. The rubble on the near corner would have been the remains of number 54, where William Tyers lived.

Manor Road from the opposite direction. The houses in the distance on the right are on the far side of the junction with Belgrave Street, with the tower of the Memorial Church just beyond them.

One of many roads in Wallasey hit during the Christmas Blitz was Eastcroft Road in Poulton. One bomb landed on or near numbers 16-20, doing quite serious damage. At number 18, a woman called Martha Carter was injured on 20 December 1940. She was taken to Mill Lane Hospital, but died the same day. This suggests the raid of 20/21 December 1940 since there was no enemy activity on the previous night.

Houses on the opposite side of the road were also damaged, probably by the same blast because the damage here is mostly confined to broken windows and doors. This image shows damage to numbers 9-15.

Heavy damage to 69 and 71 Dalmorton Road, Wallasey on the night of 20/21 December 1940. Roads like this one, being close to the river tended to suffer more hits than others. Unfortunately in this case the heavy damage reflected the casualties inflicted, with four people losing their lives here.

In Dalmorton Road, 28-year-old Majorie Cain was killed at number 69, whilst the Finn family, consisting of Ernest, his wife Winifred and their 11-month-old son George were all killed next door at number 71.

21/22 December 1940

The longest night of the year also saw the most extensive raid to date, lasting from 6.38 pm until 5.15 am. The damage was correspondingly severe and widespread. The raid began mostly with incendiaries, which started fierce fires in several areas of Liverpool.

High Explosives soon followed, with notable incidents at St George's Hall, the Fish Market in Great Charlotte Street, Hatton Garden, an electric station in Highfield Street and Hanover Street, where the premises of Ayrton Saunders was hit. Beneath both St George's Hall and the Fish Market, people were sheltering from the air raids and they had to be moved whilst bombs were still falling around them due to the danger from the fires started in each structure.

A bomb struck the St Anthony's School shelter, where eleven people died, two of them priests. Near Prescot Street Police station, a parachute mine exploded, damaging the station and a nearby bedding factory. Other mines hit the Royal Infirmary and several residential areas throughout the city. Damage was also done to Canada, Gladstone, Brocklebank, Princes, Wapping, Kings and Carriers Docks. Following two nights of heavy raids the city was burning fiercely, and around 1,200 Auxiliary Fire Service staff were brought in from other cities and towns to help.

No less than twenty-four high explosives are recorded as landing in the borough of Bootle on this night, along with numerous incendiaries. At Akenside Street, forty houses were demolished, eighteen badly damaged and eighty slightly. Another device landed on Ivanhoe Street, demolishing twenty houses and damaging another seven. Sidney Road was also badly affected, with seven houses demolished, eight badly damaged and forty- six slightly damaged.

Other roads badly hit were Anglesey Street, Berry Street, Pembroke Road and Breeze Hill. Aside from residential properties, the County Hall in Pembroke Road was targetted. This housed the food office, which held the ration books for a large part of the borough, most of which were destroyed in the resulting fire. The parish church of Bootle, St Mary's was gutted by fire, damage that it would never recover from. The site is now a memorial gardens, with a stone in the centre to remind people of the church's sad demise. Rootes Timber Yard, Lamb's Timber Yard, both on Pacific Road, Campbell and Isherwood's in Raleigh Street and Blackledge's Bakery were all also hit.

The premises of Campbell and Isherwood on Raleigh Street in Bootle, damaged during the raid of 21/22 December 1940. This view looks towards Derby Road and away from Regent Road and the docks.

Those residents of Viola Street who survived the previous night's damage would most likely have been evacuated shortly afterwards. Any that remained, however, would have been horrified to see a parachute mine landing in their road for the second night running. Fortunately this one failed to explode and was eventually made safe, and then removed.

Crosby came under more serious attack than ever before. Twenty-three high explosive bombs were scattered across the borough, with two parachute mines landing and exploding and another two unexploded mines landing. One of these, which landed on St Michael's Road, caused a three day evacuation whilst it was being dealt with. There were also twelve incidents involving incendiaries.

A total of ten people were killed and thirty-one were injured in the raid on Crosby. Nine houses were demolished, forty-eight were seriously damaged and at least 300 were slightly damaged.

It may have escaped damage on the previous night, but Birkenhead was not to be so lucky for a second time. The authorities recorded eighty-five incidents, split roughly evenly between incendiaries and high explosives. Extensive damage was done to the town centre, whilst other bombs landed on Bidston, Greasby, Bebington, Little Sutton, Claughton and Higher Tranmere.

The dock estate was also hammered, with two ships berthed there struck. There were fires at Mortar Mill Quay and damage was done to Cavendish Wharf, Spillers Flour Mills, Rank Flour Mills, Morpeth Dock, Woodside Lairage and the LMS Railway Goods Shed. There were also reports of Cammell Laird and Clovers being hit. Other notable incidents included a bomb hitting the Ritz Cinema on Claughton Road, killing five people and another landing in Laird Street, where six people were killed in a tram shelter. Initial reports gave the number of fatalities as sixteen and around eighty injuries, many of whom were trapped.

St Aidan's Terrace, off Shrewbsury Road, Oxton, Birkenhead, thought to have been damaged in the raid of 21/22 December 1940. Despite the damage, the building remains standing to this day.

Damage to numbers 91-95 Shrewsbury Road, Oxton, Birkenhead, seems to have been confined to the exterior walls of the property, although it seems likely the windows were broken in the raid as the residents have boarded most of them up. This damage is known to have been done during the raid of 21/22 December 1940. As these houses are opposite St Aidan's Terrace (previous page) it is presumed that the damage occurred at the same time.

The Grove Cafe, on the corner of Grove Road and Wallasey Village, Wallasey. As with so much of the damage done during the Christmas Blitz, the exact night this was inflicted on is unknown. Grove Road is in the foreground, whilst Wallasey Village (the road) is in the distance. The approach to Wallasey Grove Road station is just visible on the right. Windsors Garage (see page 57) is also just out of shot on the right.

The original St Peter and Paul Church, New Brighton, on the corner of Rowson Street and Hope Street. Replaced by a larger church (known to wartime sailors as the Dome from Home) that was built in the 1930s, this building was burnt out during the Christmas Blitz. The site, like so many others is now a car park. Somewhat surprisingly, despite its prominent position and large size, the newer church appears to have escaped without any serious damage during the raids, although several bombs did fall close by, such as in Sandringham Drive.

In common with the rest of the region, Wallasey's civil defences were under a great deal of pressure during the Christmas Blitz. The night must have seemed almost endless for the workers who were tasked with fighting fires, rescue work, dealing with those made homeless by the raids and treating the injured.

The borough was divided into groups, with each responsible for a specific area. Group 9, which covered much of Wallasey Village, had so far been fortunate. As its location was furthest from the river, this sheltered it from enemy bombs. This raid was therefore the group's first real experience of serious enemy action, with bombs hitting residential property on Radstock, Probyn and Russell Roads, but also commercial buildings such as the Windsor's Garage on Grove Road.

Damage to properties at the corner of Leasowe Road (in the foreground) and Probyn Road done on the night of 21/22 December 1940. Despite the extensive damage done to this corner property, nobody was killed in either road on that night. Although this was Leasowe Road's first experience of bombs, it would certainly not be its last, with the road also badly hit during the March Blitz when houses between 12 and 24 (near the junction with Wallasey Village) were badly damaged.

The rear of Windsors Garage badly damaged in the raid of 21/22 December 1940. Although hard to make out, at least two cars are just visible on the upper floor.

Damage to Russell Road in Wallasey Village caused during the air raid of 21/22 December 1940. The rubble on the left is the remains of houses which do not appear to have been rebuilt after the war as the land is empty.

Despite their lack of direct experience, the authorities were later able to report that the wardens and other civil defence workers had dealt with the situation admirably. Their ability and bravery undoubtedly saved many lives.

After suffering further damage, including broken windows along with a loss of gas, electricity and water, Victoria Central Hospital (then known as Mill Lane Hospital) on Mill Lane was evacuated during the December Blitz. This delicate but necessary operation would have been very difficult given the fragile state of the patients, combined with the cold weather. It did not reopen for another three weeks.

The hospital seems to have been particularly unlucky as it was also badly damaged during the May Blitz when a parachute mine got hung up in a tree nearby, and it had to be evacuated on that occasion too. For a site not particularly close to the river, this level of damage was unusual.

Above left: A high explosive bomb exploded in the middle of Brougham Road, Seacombe, Wallasey during the Christmas Blitz. A car that would have been parked in the road was thrown up into the air and came to rest between the doorway of number 32 and the boundary wall.

Although no doubt an inconvenience, the owners of the nearby properties could count themselves lucky that the bomb struck the road rather than their house.

Above right: Close up view of the same, showing more detail. In other photographs taken at the time, children have come to see the spectacle. The sight of a bomb damaged road or house would be unlikely to have drawn their attention, but the overturned car may well have done. It is also interesting to note that at least one of these photographs is labelled as 8 January 1941, two weeks after the raids in which the damage was done.

Heavy damage to properties in Croxteth Avenue, Liscard, Wallasey done during the Christmas Blitz. The men in the photograph seem to be recovering possessions from the houses, hence the use of handcarts. At this time, fuel shortages through rationing made using cars or trucks for this role difficult.

Number 53 Leominster Road, demolished by bombs during the Christmas Blitz.

Left: Chatsworth Avenue, Wallasey showing the heavy damage done to properties between numbers 7 and 11. This was originally thought to show numbers 1-7 and was recorded as such in Merseyside Blitzed, however research and a study of the modern properties has provided the correct numbers.

Below: The opposite side of Chatsworth Avenue showing damage to houses from numbers 12 to 2.

22/23 DECEMBER 1940

For the third consecutive night, Merseyside was hammered with bombs. In Liverpool, Medlock Street and Ensor Street were hit as were Huskisson and Canada Dock, whilst the Rootes factory took a direct hit from a high explosive, killing one person and injuring three.

Bootle also came under attack, with Langton Dock and Alexandra Dock hit. Four high explosives were dropped on the town, landing in the following places: the junction of Malvern Road and Markfield Road, the junction of Marsh Lane and Malta Road, near to Carolina and Oregon Street and the railway near Kings Road, closing the line between Seaforth and Liverpool for several days.

In Crosby, two high explosive bombs landed on Cambridge Road, one landed on Waterloo Road and eight landed in fields in the Little Crosby area.

Wallasey saw a small number of high explosives scattering across the borough, but they did little harm in comparison to the damage of the previous two nights.

Although the raid's length was no shorter, there were far fewer planes overhead and consequently less damage was done. It was not immediately clear as to why this was the case, but it soon became apparent that Manchester had suffered heavy damage on this night, and would do so again on the next.

Air raid damage to numbers 6-10 Florence Road, Seacombe, Wallasey on the night of 22/23 December 1940. Three people lost their lives at number 8: Joan Stark who was thirteen, Joseph Towers who was 72 and his wife Sarah Towers who was 71.

Left: Heavy damage to Mount Pleasant Road in Wallasey. The rubble in the middle of the photograph is on the corner of Pleasant Street, close to number 2 where Florence and Robert Turner lost their lives on 21 December 1940. Garages have since been built in the area.

Below: Damage to numbers 37 and 39 Barrington Road, Wallasey as seen from the corner of Gorsebank Street. Horse drawn carts such as the one just visible on the left would have been a common sight around the region during the blitz due to petrol rationing.

27 DECEMBER 1940

Just after 10.00 am, eight high explosives landed in fields in the Little Crosby area, followed by a single high explosive which hit a farm shed in Delph Road. At around the same time, seven incendiaries landed in woods. No damage was recorded for any of these incidents.

The house of Francis W Apperley, which stood on the corner of Rowson Street and Pickering Street, was bombed during the December raids.

Following publication of *Merseyside Blitzed* I was contacted by a relative of his who corrected some of the details I had given and provided the following information.

'He began his motor business after the First World War, and as a qualified engineer (as were his two sons), not only bought, sold, and serviced quality motor cars, but was a prominent member of Wallasey Town Council, serving some eight years, and also president of both the Motor Trade and Motor Agent's Association, and the Institute of Motor Traders.

During the Second World War, Francis Apperley and his two sons ran a full time engineering business from the machine shops on Pickering Rd, producing pieces for Mather and Platt, Manchester, and parts for aircraft, ships, guns and torpedoes for the Government. The house did take a direct hit, but the garage and machine workshops were not affected, and operated twenty-four hours a day for nearly three years.

After the war, they continued their motor business, and the machine shops produced parts for motor manufacturers, including Rolls Royce, Bentley, Riley, and Wolsley cars. The site of the bombed house eventually became a Shell petrol station. This was owned by William A. Apperley until the late 1970s, when he retired.'

New Year Raids,
January to April 1941

The run up to Christmas was a terrifying and difficult time for most people on Merseyside, but the pattern in the enemy's attacks was clearly changing. During the early raids, the attacks were frequent but limited in scope, but from December onwards, short periods of heavy enemy activity would rudely shatter any periods of relative calm.

The often long and baffling gaps in the enemy's assault against the region must have been welcome but also rather destabilizing. They gave people time to recover, but could sometimes lead to a false sense of security. The Luftwaffe simply lacked sufficient bombers to carry out regular strikes against all the targets it wished to hit, so many cities found themselves suffering from the same sporadic pattern of attacks. Unaware of the enemy's priorities or limitations, it must have seemed as if the Luftwaffe was simply toying with them.

For most people on the Wirral, March and *not* May 1941 was the worst month of the entire war, with Birkenhead losing 228 of its citizens and Wallasey 189 nine. (The figures for May were twenty-eight and three respectively.) Large swathes of both boroughs were severely damaged. Within a few days, the authorities were reporting that 2,500 houses in Birkenhead and 7,400 in Wallasey were either destroyed or rendered 'unfit for habitation'. Again, these fell mostly in a three-day period, which would have made the impact of the raids seem that much greater.

In addition to the homeless problem, both boroughs also suffered from their own particular issues. In Wallasey, the main services took a serious battering, with a report compiled on the 16 March stating that the gas supply was not expected to be restored for three days and the water until the following afternoon. The same report stated that the digging of field latrines (toilets) had been authorized due to the lack of water. An earlier report compiled in the midst of the raids (at 6.00 am on 13 March) warned of a total stoppage of electricity, which would prevent the use of air raid sirens until it was restored. This could have had catastrophic consequences for the local population had they been caught unawares, unable to take shelter during the raids that followed.

Birkenhead meanwhile considered the situation dire enough to call for the assistance of 300 military personnel to assist with search and rescue work. Although undoubtedly necessary, the presence of so many troops on the streets could sometimes have a negative effect on morale, as was later illustrated during the May Blitz when rumours flew around that the city was under martial law, with thousands dead and some residents hanging white flags of surrender from their windows. Despite many of these tales being demonstrably false, the wartime air of secrecy lead many to leap to their own conclusions.

Although the Wirral suffered more from these raids, Liverpool, Bootle and Crosby did not escape unscathed. In the minds of people today and perhaps in the memories of those who lived through the events, what was to follow in May 1941 was so horrific that it may well have made even these hugely damaging attacks seem minor in comparison.

1/2 JANUARY 1941

As if starting as they meant to go on, the Luftwaffe returned to the skies over Liverpool. A sack warehouse in Redcross Street was demolished by high explosives, killing one person and trapping two. High Explosives and a parachute mine landed in the river near Brunswick Dock and damage was also done to Mercer Court.

3/4 JANUARY 1941

A lone raider passed over Liverpool. Incendiaries fell on the Sandforth Road area and the Newsham Park allotments. The only damage done was to a stable in Sandforth Road, but even here the police reported that the fire was relatively small.

Meanwhile, over in Wallasey, a single bomb landed in the Navy League grounds in Withens Lane. The authorities stated that it was the heaviest calibre bomb that the German's had in their arsenal. The crater it blew was about 65ft across and the bomb had penetrated nearly 20ft before exploding. Fortunately nobody was killed in the incident.

9/10 JANUARY 1941

Liverpool was hit again, this time with much more force. The raiders primarily concentrated on the docks area, with high explosives falling on South Herculaneum Dock and the Dingle Oil Depot, although some bombs also fell on Gladstone Dock at the other end of the dock estate.

Slight fires were caused in the Everton area by incendiaries, mostly affecting houses although the Police Stores in Everton Terrace were hit by one that did some damage to the uniforms stored there. A barn was also set on fire at Holt Farm, Gateacre.

Elsewhere high explosives slammed into Virgil Street, seriously damaging many of the houses in the street. Many homes were also struck in the area around the junction of Lorenzo Drive and Broad Lane, whilst high explosives landed in Alexandra Drive in Dingle, causing some casualties. Later reports gave casualties for Liverpool alone as twenty-seven dead, thirteen seriously injured and forty-three slightly injured.

In Crosby, four high explosives came to earth, with one landing on Alexandra Park, two on the Serpentine and one on the foreshore near Burbo Bank Road. Two people were injured and several houses suffered minor damage, but luckily nobody was killed.

Birkenhead received its own heavy toll of bombs, with at least twenty-four high explosives and eleven incidents of incendiary bombs being recorded, along with three unexploded bomb incidents. This may not sound like very many but the damage done to the borough was widespread and considerable. It would be impossible to list all the roads hit during the raid, but bombs were scattered across the whole borough, with the town centre, Claughton, Oxton, Prenton, Rock Ferry, Tranmere, Barnston, Pensby and Bidston areas all hit.

Wallasey also caught its fair share of bombs, with incidents recorded at Sandringham Drive, Albion Street, Atherton Street, Wallasey Road, Creek Side, Pennine Road, Warrens Yard and the Dock Road. Two people in the borough were killed in the raid, one was seriously injured and eight were slightly hurt.

8/9 FEBRUARY 1941

The authorities reported that an unexploded bomb was discovered in Kings Lane, Rock Ferry. Exactly when it was dropped was unknown, but it was presumably disposed of safely as there is no mention of an explosion.

12/13 FEBRUARY 1941

This night saw a harsh raid on Birkenhead, with bombs landing on Lord Street, Cathcart Street, Mallaby Street, Neston Street and Watson Street. The rest of the region appears to have escaped damage.

15/16 FEBRUARY 1941

Two separate raids occurred, the first lasting just thirty minutes, in which bombs fell on Aigburth and Garston, but the damage was slight. The second lasted for two hours and hit northern parts of the city, with both high explosives and incendiaries falling. A Post Office garage on Commercial Road was damaged.

In Bootle, the raiders dropped a hail of incendiaries, hitting Wadham Road, Bedford Road, Beatrice Street, Benedict Street, Olivia Street, Miranda Road and parts of Stanley Road. As was often the case with this kind of device, when they landed in a residential area, the damage was slight.

19/20 FEBRUARY 1941

In another isolated raid, bombs fell on Well Lane in Tranmere.

20/21 FEBRUARY 1941

Bombs fell on Egerton Dock, although no description is given for how bad the damage was.

Although little obvious damage seems to have been done to Martins Lane, Wallasey in this photograph, it is nonetheless interesting to note the water pipe running along the gutter. Wallasey was to suffer from problems with water pressure during the March 1941 blitz. The authorities often responded to such problems by the pumping of water from the docks or other places like Central Park's Lake. The photo is undated, but may have been taken in early 1941.

24/25 FEBRUARY 1941

Birkenhead was once again the sole target of the raiders, with bombs falling on Bidston Hill, Boundary Road, Duke Street near Park Station and Beckwith Street.

12/13 MARCH 1941

After a break of more than a fortnight, the raiders returned to the skies over Merseyside to inflict severe damage over a three day period..

In Liverpool, a heavy attack battered the city, starting 126 separate fires. The scale of the attack was such that outside fire brigades were called in to assist with the conflagration. The authorities had also called for assistance from the military and a number of soldiers were also present in the city on fire watching duties.

Liverpool's vital communications took several blows during this raid. The Head Post Office building on Victoria Street was hit by incendiaries which started a major fire, burning out two floors. Considerable damage was also done by the water used in putting the fire out, which was a common problem. Incendiaries also caused fire damage to the White Star Line building, Athol Street Gasworks, St Mary's Church on Highfield Street and the Cotton Exchange on Old Hall Street.

Meanwhile, the central telephone exchange on South John Street was evacuated after a parachute mine came to earth in nearby Atherton Street, followed by a second nearby. The authorities had naturally planned for this eventuality and had a backup exchange set up in Lancaster House, but this too was hit by a high explosive bomb shortly afterwards. Fortunately, that device did not do any damage to the exchange so it was still able to take over the work.

Heavy damage to a property at the junction of St Hilary Brow and Breck Road, Wallasey inflicted during the March Blitz. The twin towers of St Hillary's Church can be made out to the left of the battered house.

A mine which landed in Atherton Street came down in the middle of a fire. When it exploded, it killed two 18-year-olds, one a fire watcher and the other a member of the Home Guard. The explosion also damaged surrounding properties by spreading the fire, making the damage from this one device even worse. Other major incidents caused by mines included St Anne's School in Chatham Place, Great Crosshall Street and Lace Street. At the latter, around a dozen people from the old tenements in the street were killed.

The victims of the St Anne's school incident were particularly unfortunate. It started when a mine came down on the school, causing civil defence workers to rush to the area and evacuate nearby shelters. Whilst this was going on, a high explosive came down nearby and set off the mine, killing many of the workers.

Many streets in the Everton and Walton areas were hit by high explosives, as was the Engineering department of the University, the Liverpool Stadium and the overhead railway on Regent Road.

Bootle was also hit, in the Rimrose Road and Seaforth Street area, with St Winefride's School, a large laundry and one house set on fire. The high explosives which followed, damaged houses in Canal Street, a large warehouse in Benbow Street, Taylor's timber yard in Regent Road, offices and flats in Regent Road, the overhead electricity wires for the overhead railway, and the Langton Castle Hotel.

In Crosby, sixteen people were killed and thirty-one injured in a raid. The worst incident occurred at Sandy Road in Seaforth where a parachute mine exploded, devastating the houses nearby and causing the fatalities. Another parachute mine landed on allotments near Sandy Road but failed to explode, and two hit Rosemoor Drive, one of which also failed to go off.

Heavy damage to properties on the corner of Duke Street and Beckwith Street, Birkenhead. This was inflicted during the March Blitz.

Right: Slight damage done to the District Bank in Wallasey during the March blitz. The building stood on the corner of Church Road and Brighton Street. Most of the structure has remained intact, but the windows and doors have been destroyed. The branch moved temporarily to Brighton Street.

Below: Heavy damage done to the Earlston Road Library in Wallasey during the March Blitz. Of particular interest are the two signs on the fence, one of which points the way to a shelter (also damaged during these raids) whilst the other notes that the building was the site of ARP Warden Post 3a. Such posts were often located in large public buildings such as this one. Luckily none of the wardens were killed or injured in the incident and could continue their good work.

Mallaby Street, seen from the junction with Park Road North. In the distance is the Laird Street Bus Depot.

Across the borough of Crosby, eight houses were demolished, thirty-seven were seriously impacted and more than 200 were lightly damaged.

But it was the Wirral that suffered the worst damage with Wallasey and Birkenhead suffering the most. The sheer number of incidents and roads hit make it impossible to list them all, so what follows is a summary of the most notable incidents.

In Birkenhead, a large swathe of Brattan Road was flattened by a parachute mine, killing thirteen people. The incident was considered of such interest that when the Prime Minister, Winston Churchill came to visit the borough the following month, he stopped in the road to sign the Birkenhead visitors' book on a table set out for his visit.

Mallaby Street and the Corporation Depot on Laird Street were both hit, with seven men killed and eight buses written off and 136 others less seriously damaged. The Avenue Cinema was seriously damaged, with two people losing their lives nearby. On the corner of Cleveland Street and Cathcart Street, the Caledonia Hotel was struck, killing eleven. The station buildings of Birkenhead Park Station were badly damaged. In Price Street, seven people lost their lives, whilst in Laird Street, between the junctions with Lansdowne Road and Miriam Place, more than twenty people were killed. At Euston Grove, six people died, whilst in Well Lane nearly thirty people were killed.

Our Lady's Roman Catholic Church on the corner of Price Street and Cavendish Street was badly damaged, as was part of St Saviour's Church in Oxton. Hardly any part of the borough was untouched by the raid, the effects of which were so great that the authorities called for and received support from other nearby towns. This took the form of rescue parties and mobile canteens, the latter essential in feeding the many people made homeless by the raids. They also called for the support of 300 military staff to help in the short-term whilst civilian labour was organized.

The serious damage done to the Avenue Cinema was later to lead to its demolition. Even the public house seen here is closed at the time of writing.

Houses in Laird Street flattened during the March Blitz. The site is now occupied by advertising hoardings.

The Canada Hotel on the corner of Price Street and Old Bidston Road was devastated on the night of 12/13 March 1941. It is now the site of a school playground. On the right, the rear of Our Lady's Roman Catholic Church can be seen.

This crossing area is well used as it connects Birkenhead Central Station to the town's main shopping area, however many who pass by will have no idea that just the other side of the high wall was once a scene of destruction. Immediately after the raid, the roadway to the right was blocked off, perhaps due to the damage or an unexploded bomb.

The premises of Hubbard and Martin's Electric Bakery on Pilgrim Street, Birkenhead was badly damaged during the March Blitz, with the entrance way and roof damaged. The street itself has also been cratered and five men are hard at work carrying out repairs. A gang of children and a dog have also gathered to watch the men work. It is hard to imagine them being allowed to stand so close to a clearly dangerous wall in this modern age!

These houses on Whetstone Lane in Birkenhead had their windows and doors blown out in the March Blitz, although they remained largely intact and were able to be repaired. A small workman's hut has been erected in front of the house on the left and a barrier ran around the building in an effort to keep people from entering. Compared to many people in Birkenhead, the owners could count themselves lucky that the damage was not worse.

A parachute mine exploded near this spot during the March raids, at the rear of houses on Bolton Road, Port Sunlight. On the right part of the Employees Central Stores building (which also housed the Collegium and Mac Fisheries) can also be seen. Numbers 14-18 Bolton Road, and 8-14 Bridge Street (the latter out of shot on the left) were either demolished outright or pulled down later. Apart from the Employees Central Stores building (the site of which is still empty today), the properties would be rebuilt in a style that is in keeping with the rest of the village.

Left: Light damage to houses in Daffodil Road, Claughton after the raid on 12/13 March 1941. Compared to the December raids, when number 32 was utterly demolished and a family of three were killed, the residents could consider themselves lucky.

Below: Damage to Harcourt Street, Birkenhead seen from Duke Street following the March Blitz. Nearby Birkenhead Park station was badly damaged in the same raid. The bombing probably also damaged nearby gas mains as a temporary sign was put up warning people not to smoke or light up. Burst gas mains were a regular problem for the authorities to tackle as they could hinder rescue operations and should the gas catch fire, this would cause much more damage than the initial bomb.

Wallasey was also severely damaged by this raid and others on the subsequent two nights. With so many incidents in such a short space of time, it is difficult to trace what damage occurred on each, and it is easier to simply attribute them all to the March Blitz. Most of the borough suffered damage of some sort from the eight parachute mines and 148 high explosives that fell on the area.

Claremount Road was very badly hit, with six people losing their lives. At Erskine Road, around a dozen people were killed, including an Air Raid Warden who was carrying out his duties there. One side of the road was also all but demolished and the other badly damaged.

At Lancaster Avenue, a parachute mine destroyed much of the housing near the junction with Wimbledon Street, and killed around thirty people between the two. Sometime on 16 March, workers were clearing away rubble in this area when they heard the faint cries of a child. Working with great care they managed to clear a safe route to the noise and found a tiny baby girl, somehow sheltered by the bodies of her parents. She was rescued and taken to Victoria Central Hospital, where she made an amazing recovery. To the rescuers, the remarkable survival of this child, who was only a few months old at the time of the raid, must have seemed a welcome miracle in such a sea of tragedy.

The damage to 117 and 119 Rake Lane during the March Blitz, Wallasey was so serious that neither remain standing today. On the left is the edge of Rake Lane Cemetery where there is a memorial to those who fell during the air raids.

Two views of the damage to properties on the corner of Adelaide Street and Norwood Road, Poulton, Wallasey. The view above looks towards Norwood Road, whilst that below is from Norwood Road.

Serious as it seems to our modern eyes, there was no loss of life here during the March Blitz raids which caused such devastation. Even so, the residents of these houses would have had their lives changed forever.

Also probably hit during the March Blitz raids were numbers 64-50 Norwood Road, with many demolished. Although photographs of the incident are given the date of 31 March 1941 in the archive's records, a study of the Civilian Roll of Honour shows that four people are listed as falling on 13 March 1941, two each at numbers 60 and 62. This then is the most likely date.

At some point, an unexploded bomb must also have been found in the road as these men from a bomb disposal squad were photographed posing proudly with the defused device outside number 64. Their relief at making another deadly bomb safe can clearly be seen. This was an extremely dangerous role, and many squad members were killed performing this essential task. Without the hard work of men like these, the damage of the blitz would have been even greater.

Church Street was devastated, with fourteen people dying and large areas of housing destroyed. The street's First Aid depot was damaged, but remained open during the raids. The Mill Lane Hospital was evacuated again due to a failure of the gas, mains and water supplies. Poulton Road was also hit, with Poulton School suffering particularly heavy damage. The electricity supply to the borough stopped for a short period, gas production ceased for several days and the water supply was limited due to damage to the mains causing pressure problems.

Wartime demolition and modern day repair work on Northbrook Road, Wallasey (just off Poulton Road). A nearby chapel was also badly damaged. The area on the left is now part of a school playground, hence the road markings.

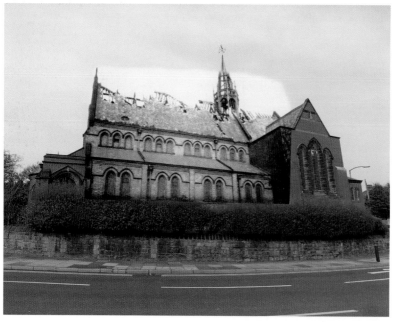

St Luke's Church on Poulton Road was also hit during the March Blitz. The roof and steeple were badly damaged by fire, despite the efforts of local people. As the flames were in an inaccessible location, they had to abandon the task and try to save interior fittings, including the church pews. The building was later repaired and reopened in the 1950s.

Elsewhere on the Wirral, Rock Park, Harley Avenue, Pulford Road, Thornton Road, Bolton Road East, Town Lane and Victoria Park in Bebington were all hit. No less than seven high explosives landed in the Lever Brothers Works in Port Sunlight, fortunately doing no major damage. Elsewhere in Port Sunlight, village houses in Church Drive and Bolton Road were hit. The Mayfield area in New Ferry suffered damage from two parachute mines, with seventeen houses wrecked and three people killed. In Bromborough, several houses were demolished and shops damaged, whilst a parachute mine damaged the roof and windows of the Brotherton Chemical works. Bombs fell on Barnston causing six slight casualties, whilst Gayton and Storeton were both struck by high explosives.

This depicts bomb damage to houses at the junction of Harley Avenue and Thornton Road, Bebington. They were hit during the raid on 12/13 March 1941. The nearest property was later rebuilt but those in the background on Thornton Avenue appear to have been repaired and show no obvious trace of the damage seen here.

Several Houses on Colville Road were demolished or damaged during the March Blitz. This is the view from the junction with Wallasey Road.

13/14 MARCH 1941

The raiders returned on a smaller scale. Over in Liverpool, bombs fell on the shoreline at Garston. Two ships sank in the river after hitting mines, whilst some slight damage was done to the rest of the city.

In Bootle, Alexandra Dock was hit by high explosives and incendiaries, with dock sheds hit. The only damage to the town itself was self-inflicted when an anti-aircraft shell came to earth in Denbigh Street, damaging two houses. Over in Crosby, a parachute mine landed between Gladstone Dock and Lambs Timber Yard, whilst eleven high explosives were scattered across the rest of the borough, hitting the Methodist Church on Mersey Road, Warwick Avenue, Earl's Close and Blundellsands Road East.

In Birkenhead, bombs are believed to have fallen on Mona Street, Devonshire Road and Bridge Street, all doing slight damage. Two devices also fell in Hamilton Square's gardens, luckily missing the houses but shattering many of the square's windows.

Some sources give the dates for the damage in the photographs on the following page as 12/13 March 1941, others 13/14 March 1941. It is often difficult to be certain after the passage of more than seven decades, especially as those responsible for recording the information would have been under great stress, so could be forgiven any mistakes. What can be said for certain is that two deaths were recorded for Mona Street for 12 March 1941 suggesting some bombs fell there on the first night.

One of the victims of 13/14 March 1941 raid was the Methodist Church in Mersey Road, Crosby. The church frontage was altered after the raid when the borough pulled down the spire and part of the tower, presumably as it may have been in a dangerous condition due to the damage. The building remains standing today, albeit with a more symmetrical frontage. The workmen near the modern 4x4 seem to be repairing the roadway, which is known to have been blocked through damage in the same raid.

This shows slight damage to Numbers 2-4 Devonshire Road, Claughton. During the war, these buildings were the premises of George Bolton's garage and taxi firm on Birkenhead. The damage appears to be minor and for the most part confined to the gates in the centre of the image.

Mona Street, Claughton, hit during the March Blitz. Given how short and narrow the road is, it is really quite remarkable that it seems to have survived the raids without any serious damage. This suggests a small device landed in the area.

A view along the devastated section of Wallasey Village, looking towards the junction with Leasowe Road. Clear up work has already begun, but given the scale of the damage is likely to last some time yet.

17 and 19 Lynwood Avenue, Wallasey, another set of houses destroyed at some point during the March Blitz.

Wallasey bore a heavy burden, with no less than five air raid wardens losing their lives overnight, whilst both the head warden and his deputy were also injured. The Coliseum Picturedrome was gutted by fire. It was later demolished, and a post-war cinema was built on the site with the apt name of The Phoenix. In many places, a water shortage meant the fires were incredibly hard to bring under control.

14/15 MARCH 1941
The final night of the March Blitz saw a small raid on Liverpool, with one device landing on the railway line near Walton Hospital, and others landing on houses in Melrose Road, Argos Road and Tees Street in Kirkdale. Around 200 incendiaries also landed in the Speke area of the city.

Wallasey also saw bombs land in Central Park Avenue, Eaton Avenue and Somerville School. Casualties were light, especially in comparison to the raid of two nights earlier.

1-3 Daresbury Road, Wallasey, as seen from the junction with Rullerton Road. Several items of furniture have been salvaged from the mess. In another closer photograph taken at the same time, it is possible to see that an ironing board, table and some drawers were amongst the items saved.

Both of these photographs were taken around the same time and probably represent damage done on the same night during the March Blitz as they are almost opposite each other.

The shattered remains of the wartime 56 and 58 Rullerton Road merge with the modern view. Also of interest is the pre-war style sign (to the left of the modern lamppost) saying, 'Halt at major road ahead'. This is presumably a reference to Mill Lane. Mill Lane Water Tower can just be seen on the right.

Men working on repairing Grove Road, Wallasey, after it was damaged during the March raids. The road to the right is St George's Road, and this view looks up Grove Road, away from Grove Road Station.

Wheatland Lane was badly bombed in the March Blitz, with several houses destroyed or damaged beyond repair. This view looks towards the junction with Poulton Road. All the housing between St Joseph's Church and the group on the right has since been demolished, and a school now occupies much of the land.

7/8 APRIL 1941

After the terrible devastation of the March Blitz there was a gap of nearly four weeks without attacks. On this night though, about twenty explosive incendiaries landed in the Beaconsfield Road area, 150 incendiaries landed in Garston and another 200 fell in the Menlove Avenue area. High explosives followed, landing near Kirkdale Railway Station, damaging railway coaches and the line itself. A convent on Edge Lane was hit and damaged, as was the attached chapel. Other places hit included Lister Drive, the Old Swan district, Woolton Road and Lilley Road in Fairfield.

Meanwhile in Bebington, pine woods along Storeton Ridge caught fire, bombs also fell in the Kings Lane Allotments and the Woodhey area. In the Birkenhead area, they landed in Boundary Road, Holm Lane and Powell Street.

Wallasey was struck by high explosives of a larger than normal calibre, which made it all the more fortunate that nobody was killed in the raid. The devices fell on Borrowdale Road, Joan Avenue, Eleanor Road, Serpentine Road, Hawarden Avenue, Karslake Road and Hawthorne Grove. Elsewhere on the Wirral, high explosives landed in Saughall Massie, Neston, Bromborough, Hoylake, and Greasby.

Fairly light damage was done to housing in Holm Lane, Oxton during the raid on 7/8 April 1941. One possible reason for it being targetted was that the lane contained an anti-aircraft battery.

Much of Euston Grove was badly hit in the March Blitz, but most photographs were taken from a high vantage point, (probably the upper window of a house) which is hard to match today. This is one of the few that was taken from ground level and shows the heavy damage done to houses on the corner of Euston Grove and Balfour Road. At least half a dozen people lost their lives in Euston Grove during the March raids.

This is Serpentine Road, as seen from Martins Lane after the raid on 7/8 April 1941. Numbers 92-96 have taken the brunt of the damage.

Right: Also damaged in the raid of 7/8 April 1941 were the properties 19-25 Hawarden Avenue, Wallasey. This image shows the damage from Empress Road, with the remains of number 25 nearest to the camera. Considering how much damage has been done here, it is really rather remarkable that nobody was killed nearby.

Below: Another view of the incident at Hawarden Avenue, this time showing the damage to numbers 19 and 21. Despite appearing relatively intact it seems likely that number 19 was either demolished or significantly altered after the raids, since the layout of the modern building is quite different. The road on the left is Ferndale Avenue.

15/16 APRIL 1941

In the initial attack on Liverpool, Garston and Aigburth came under attack from explosive incendiaries. High explosives followed, demolishing 42 and 44 Saunby Street in Garston, where eight people died. Bryant and May's Garston Factory, Blackwell's Metalurgical works and Rawlinson's Timber Merchants were also hit.

Other houses nearby were also damaged. Later that night, high explosives also landed in the Great Homer Street area, doing considerable damage to nearby houses. Other places affected in the raid included Gladstone Dock, the Litherland Rubber Works, Langrove Street, Opie Street and Arkwright Street.

Bootle also came under attack again. Incendiaries fell in the St Andrew's Road, Halsall Road and Hawthorne Road areas, damaging houses and a bus company's garage. Two houses in Coleridge Street were demolished and twenty-seven were damaged when a high explosive bomb landed there. Another high explosive landed on Robinson and Co's premises on Knowsley Road, and a third landed in Rimrose Street, damaging a timber yard. St Andrew's Church Hall roof and eight houses in Litherland Road were also hit. One person was killed, two seriously injured and sixteen slightly injured.

Crosby was hammered by both high explosives and a shower of incendiaries, with at least seven of the former going off and causing considerable damage. Eight people were killed and another eight were injured, whilst three houses were demolished and eight were badly damaged.

In Birkenhead, bombs landed in Collin Road in the Bidston area, killing nineteen people.

This depicts the devastated properties on the corner of Rimrose Road (foreground) and Browning Road, Bootle. They were badly damaged during the raid on 15/16 April 1941.

This wartime image was taken in Wallasey and shows the Prime Minister being driven along the Dock Road in Wallasey. In the background, the Swan Hotel can just be made out. Despite being hit during the blitz, the building survived the raids and still stands at the time of writing, although it has been empty for some time.

25 APRIL 1941

The Prime Minister, Winston Churchill paid a visit to the area. He stopped in Birkenhead, Wallasey and Liverpool, visiting bombed out houses and talking to local residents. At least one still photograph of the visit survives along with newsreel footage.

26/27 APRIL 1941

Liverpool saw more widespread damage, most of it caused by parachute mines. These fell at Broadway, Ballantyne Road, Wayville Road, Glasonby Crescent and Pitville Road. The one which fell on the Ballantyne Road area came to earth in the grounds of Roscoe School but failed to explode, allowing the area to be evacuated. Incendiaries seem to have been scattered widely across the city without causing too many problems except at Walton Jail where they damaged the gymnasium and the chapel. The city centre escaped relatively unscathed.

Bootle came under fire from incendiary bombs, with a timber yard near to Ford Railway station damaged, as well as the factory of the International Harvester Company. Four houses were set on fire by incendiaries that penetrated their roofs. These were located in Summers Avenue, Stuart Road (one each) and Kings Avenue (two).

In Crosby, a high explosive landed on a barrage balloon base located near the shore, and incendiaries were scattered on the area between Harbord Road and Gladstone Dock. Eight people were injured and one person was killed.

In Birkenhead, incendiary bombs landed in the Upton area, whilst the King's Park Estate in Bebington and the Higher Bebington Village also had incendiaries dropped on them.

In Wallasey, two parachute mines fell in a field near to Bermuda Road in Moreton. One exploded, damaging windows and leaving a large crater, the other was later disarmed and featured in a famous photo. Incendiary bombs also fell on the village of Meols, but did little damage as they were put out promptly.

This proved to be the final raid before the terrible destruction handed out by the Luftwaffe during the May Blitz. At the time of Churchill's visit, few could have believed that within just two weeks, their city and region would be unrecognizable.

THE MAY BLITZ: MERSEYSIDE'S DARKEST HOUR

As has been alluded to several times in the course of this book, the first seven nights of May 1941 were for Merseyside the worst experience of the entire war. The Luftwaffe made several heavy raids against the area, taking advantage of the good weather and visibility to inflict massive damage to the region's port facilities, industry, transport infrastructure, shopping and business districts and of course, to its residential areas too.

It is important to stress just how difficult a period this was for the region, coming as it did within such a short space of time. Wallasey and Birkenhead had seen the nadir of their experience in the March raids, and although Liverpool, Bootle and Crosby had suffered badly in previous raids, the sheer scale of the damage in these seven nights eclipsed anything seen or heard about locally beforehand.

As has been noted earlier, this was not helped by an atmosphere of rumours and official secrecy, which tended to exaggerate the few known facts into nightmarish scenarios that bore no resemblance to reality. Many people left the city at night to head into the surrounding countryside, only to find it difficult to return the next day. Return they did though, and although morale was reported as being at a lower level than ever before, it still held. People were determined to 'do their bit' in the face of a seemingly relentless enemy.

The sheer scale of the May Blitz makes it impossible to record every single incident, even on some of the quieter nights. Although the summary ARP reports for the May Blitz are now available for viewing in the archives in Liverpool Central Library, the level of detail provided could fill a book of its own. The following will therefore naturally concentrate on the major incidents of each night. Many of these are well-known, often as stories passed down by family members who experienced them first-hand.

The impact of this short period can still be seen today for those who know where to look. The most notable example is the Liverpool One Shopping Centre, built mostly on land devastated in the May Blitz. Furthermore, whilst the number killed may seem small in comparison to the population at the time, or the raids on other cities, it must be remembered that every death represented a personal tragedy. This would have been felt keenly by the survivors, especially those serving in the armed forces, who could reasonably have expected their lives to be in greater danger than their loved ones at home.

Readers will no doubt note that this chapter is by far the longest, which is not just due to the amount of damage caused, but is also because more photographs survive from this period of the blitz than for any other. There are for example around half a dozen well-known photographs of varying quality of the Durning Road incident in November 1940, but more than twice that many of the Custom House in the aftermath of these raids.

Blitzed buildings and shattered street shelters on Fisher Street, Liverpool, in the Toxteth area of the city. This view looks from Grafton Street towards Caryl Street and the docks beyond. This former residential street is now little more than an alley.

1/2 MAY 1941

The first night of the May Blitz was comparatively quiet, but several areas across the region were hit.

In Liverpool, there was damage done to a meat factory in New Bird Street, a timber yard in Kempston Street, a shop in London Road and the glass roof of Lime Street Station. A bomb falling through the roof damaged two trains when it exploded. Travel to and from the station was also affected by unexploded bombs landing in the cutting between Overbury and Kinglake Streets.

High explosives fell on the Low Hill district, causing damage to houses. Damage was also caused to houses in Grafton Street, Fisher Street and a shed in West Brunswick Dock. Railway lines running into Garston Dock were blocked by high explosives landing in the area.

Bombs also struck houses, a bank and shops in the Cazneau Street area. The North Market was hit and damaged further (it had already been badly affected in the December Blitz) Houses on Claremont Road, Garmoyle Road and Wellington Road were demolished and there was a serious fire at Crawford's Biscuits on Binns Road.

Birkenhead's reports are a little harder to separate, with much of the damage done during the first four days in May recorded in one go. Over these four days, the impact on the borough was so widespread that it would be impossible to list all the places that were affected.

Amongst the places known to have been hit on this first night were St Vincent Road, St David Road, Howbeck Road, Vyner Road and Coniston Avenue. The railway line between Rock Ferry and Bebington Stations was also blocked by a crater caused by a high explosive landing there. The 11.33 pm train from Birkenhead to Chester ran into this crater, causing further damage and a delay in clearing the line.

Wallasey saw considerable damage to the docks, warehouses and shipping, with several severe fires started, some of which would not be completely put out for days. The situation would not have been helped by the raids which came later in the week as this provided little or no time for respite for the civil defences.

In Bebington, incendiary bombs caused slight damage to houses, whilst three high explosives landed on Bromborough Margarine Works, causing minor damage. In Neston, a single high explosive damaged a house on Boathouse Lane whilst six others landed in fields nearby. In Eastham, seven high explosives landed in a field, their explosions causing slight damage to nearby houses.

Although now a quiet area of Birkenhead, St Vincent Road in Claughton was once the scene of terrible loss of life, with at least nine people dying at either number 30 or 32. The sea of rubble that the civil defence workers are sifting through in the centre of the photograph is all that remains of the pre-war properties where so many lost their lives.

Here we can see slight damage to St David Road in Birkenheas, which occurred during the raid on the night of 1/2 May 1941. Another photograph, taken from further down the road, shows that the roadway was cratered. This explains the need for the temporary barrier which has been erected to prevent anyone from driving down the road.

2/3 MAY 1941

In Liverpool, no division was spared damage, with some incidents also singled out for special mention due to the serious fire damage they suffered. These included warehouses in Bridgewater Street, Norfolk Street and Chaloner Street. Dock sheds at the north eastern end of Queen's Dock were also affected, as was a rice mill on Upper Pownall Street, the Corn Exchange in the City Centre (started by high explosives and a shattered gas main), the White Star Building and the gas company's works on Duke Street.

A parachute mine landed on South Castle Street, doing serious damage to shops, a nearby electricity substation and two tram cars. The Dock Road was reported to be completely blocked and the overhead railway was brought crashing down.

Brunswick Street, between the Cunard Buildings and the Port of Liverpool Building (then known as the Mersey Docks and Harbour Board building) cratered by a high explosive device. This view looks towards the Cunard Buildings and in the background on the right is Tower Buildings.

High Explosives landed in Lumber Street (near Exchange Station) which did heavy damage to nearby properties and the station itself. A parachute mine landed in Cornwallis Street, doing serious damage to nearby houses. Bombs also landed on Strand Street and James Street, damaging India Buildings, the Cunard Buildings, the Mersey Docks and Harbour Board Building and the Tunnel Buildings.

Houses and shops in the areas around Upper Huskisson Street, Bedford Street, London Road and Pembroke Place were badly damaged. Parachute mines also caused heavy damage to houses on Linnet Lane, Ullet Road, Waverley Road, Mannering Road, Coltart and Kingsley Road. High explosives landed on Brunswick Goods Station, Wapping Overhead Railway Station, Grafton Street and Buckland Street.

St Brigid's Church and crypt (the latter was being used as a shelter) were both partially demolished. The rescue services acted very promptly, with seven parties arriving on the scene shortly afterwards. Of the 300 or so people present, only seven lost their lives. High explosives landed on St Athanasius' Church on Fountains Road and houses on Chancel Street. Parachute mines landed on Hunslet Road and Donsby Road along with the Railway Signal Works on Adam Crescent.

Parachute mines fell on Bowland Avenue, Maple Grove, Egerton Road, the Ministry of Pensions Hospital on Park Avenue, Ibbotsons Lane and Smithdown Road Cemetery. All of them caused severe damage. High explosives landed in Ullet Road, Glenconner Road, Childwall Valley Road, Fern Grove and Childwall Abbey Road causing serious damage. A parachute mine landed on Pemberton Road, which caused extensive damage to houses nearby and the Old Swan Police Station. Incendiary and oil bombs damaged the Automatic Telephone Company premises on Binns Road.

A report made to the Home Security Information Department on the morning of 3 May, stated that the Mersey Docks and Harbour Board had been completely destroyed. This was fortunately an exaggeration, as although damage to the upper floor and one corner of this magnificent building was quite considerable, it remained intact. This was in no small part thanks to the seventeen fire engine crews who worked so hard to fight the fires there.

This view looks along the rear of the Port of Liverpool Building (then known as the Mersey Docks and Harbour Board building) and shows men (most of whom are in uniform) inspecting the damage inflicted on it during the May Blitz. At least one parachute mine exploded nearby, starting a fire on the upper floors that was eventually contained before the damage became too serious.

The temporary sign to the left of the men informs people that the road is closed. In the distance are the Cunard Building, which also suffered a near miss during the raids. Both the Cunard and Liver Building had their lower levels converted into large shelters, with room for nearly five thousand people between them.

These two images were taken from almost the same position, standing on what is now a traffic island on the Strand, not far from the junction with James Street.

The damage to the White Star building in the photograph above was considerable, but the building was later repaired. In the photograph at the top of the page, it is possible to see that most of the properties between James Street and Brunswick Street have been demolished. The way in which the Strand is still littered with debris suggests they were taken shortly after an air raid.

Workers have turned up at the Corn Exchange on Fenwick Street only to find that their place of work has been destroyed. The wartime image was often captioned as 'Business as Usual' along with suggestions that despite their office, with all its paperwork and files being a ruin, the men in this photograph carried on working in the streets or cafes until other offices could be found for them.

This is almost the same view as the one above, but taken a short time later. By the time the wartime photograph was taken most of what little remained of the Corn Exchange has been demolished, leaving only one prominent entranceway. India Buildings is in the background on the left.

At the time of the raid, Cecil Moores, then the co-owner of Littlewoods was in the city, visiting the company's premises in Hanover Street. He decided to go onto the roof to get a better view. From there, the scene must have been appalling, and he could see the area around the company's old premises on Old Hall Street was on fire. After walking across to the site to see the blaze for himself, he returned to the Hanover Street premises (where the company made parachutes for the war effort) and ordered the night shift to return home until further notice. This was a fortunate decision, for the next night these premises were destroyed.

Exchange Station was also damaged when part of the roof was brought crashing down on the electric lines. St Michael's Church on Pitt Street was all but destroyed by a parachute mine, with only a shell and the tower remaining. The same mine also damaged the Corporation Baths on Cornwallis Street. Grayson Rollo's ship repair works on Bridgewater Street was badly damaged by high explosives and incendiaries. Near Wapping Dock, the overhead railway was brought down by another mine, with damage also done to nearby buildings and the dock wall.

Wapping Dock Warehouse and the neighbouring overhead railway after the heavy damage inflicted on both during the night of 2/3 May 1941. The warehouse had been damaged in an earlier raid and patched up, but after this one lost about a quarter of its frontage – that nearest to the camera. The overhead railway, also known as the Dockers Umbrella was a vital transport system during the war and would soon be repaired. It was demolished in the 1950s.

The view along Pitt Street, including the damage suffered by St Michael's Church on the night of 2/3 May 1941. The church would soon be demolished. Since the publication of *Liverpool Blitzed*, the former grounds have now been taken over to allow flats to be built. In the background, the tower of the then unfinished Anglican Cathedral can be made out. It was finally completed in 1978, more than seventy years after work began on it.

A badly damaged fire engine sits in Golf Links Road, Prenton. The vehicle was hit during the raid on 2/3 May 1941 outside the drive of a house known as West Hill.

Bootle suffered again, with incendiaries falling in the Cambridge Road area. A parachute mine fell near houses on Bulwer Street causing so much damage that twelve houses were demolished, thirty-four badly damaged and more than 200 slightly affected. A further mine struck Cyprus Road, with eighteen properties there demolished, three badly damaged and another 200 slightly damaged. Chadburn Telegraphs works was hit, along with the nearby Methodist hall, as well as the Public Assistance Office and Owen Peck and Co's timber yard.

Birkenhead experienced less hits than Liverpool, but the damage involved in each was still substantial. A shelter in the grounds of Woodchurch Road School was hit, with eight people killed when it collapsed. The Prenton area experienced high explosives and incendiaries, starting fires in the buildings around Prenton Lane and Golf Links Road. One of the fire engines sent to deal with the flames was destroyed. Neptune Street and Bennetts Hill were also both damaged.

Wallasey was hit with a single mine falling on New Brighton Cricket Club in Rake Lane, damaging nearby properties and injuring eleven. The foreshore was also affected by high explosives, but no damage was done.

Heavy damage to numbers 15-19 Bennetts Hill, Birkenhead inflicted during the night of 2/3 May 1941. This view looks down the hill towards Woodchurch Road. Not far away is Woodchurch Road School where eight people were killed in a shelter in the school grounds.

Perhaps the most famous victim of the May Blitz, the Lewis's department store on the corner of Ranelagh Street and Renshaw Street is seen here from Copperas Hill. This iconic landmark was burnt out during the raid on 3/4 May 1941.

3/4 MAY 1941

By far the worst raid on Merseyside of the entire war, this was a seven-hour nightmare that devastated the region, damaging a huge number of buildings and streets. It is thought that nearly 300 planes were involved in the attack, with nearly 50,000 incendiaries and 363 tons of high explosives falling on the region. It would be impossible to list all the incidents involved in the raid, and what follows is a summary of the main events.

In the city centre, Lewis's and Blackler's Stores were gutted by a fire which started in the first building and spread to the second.

The view up Ranelagh Street from near its junction with Great Charlotte Street shows more of the severe damage inflicted on this area during the May Blitz. The Vines public house, whose tower can be seen on the left was one of the few buildings nearby to come through this period without serious damage, but no doubt it would have suffered broken windows and similar.

This third view of the area highlights the damage done to the original Blackler's stores on the left. Work has already begun on the remains of the Lewis's department store in the distance, suggesting this photograph may have been taken a little while after the May Blitz. The building was partly demolished after the raids and later replaced by a modern edifice that is itself undergoing a refit at the time of writing.

Also believed to have been hit around the same time as the two nearby department stores were two of Lime Street's cinemas, the Scala (centre) and the Futurist (left). Many would later recall that the Scala was showing a film at the time entitled 'The World in Flames'. This may have seemed rather apt to locals given how many of the city's landmarks were falling victim to fire.

Strangely, some initial reports mention neither cinema and instead state that the Forum (also on Lime Street) was hit. Given the stressful situation and chaos of that night, such mistakes are understandable. Sadly, since this photograph was taken, the former Futurist cinema has been demolished as part of a development plan which will also see the demolition of the former Scala cinema building.

The fate of the two department stores was sealed shortly after midnight when a high explosive slammed into Lewis's, knocking out the sprinkler system. This was followed by oil bombs (a type of incendiary device, see glossary) and three more high explosives. Such heavy damage in a short period was difficult to cope with, especially as several fire watchers were killed around this time. The building, like many others, was soon ablaze.

Although AFS pumps rushed to the scene, they soon found that there was a water mains failure in the area. They used some quite ingenious methods to overcome the problem, including drawing water from a swimming pool in the Adelphi Hotel, but the fires still spread to nearby streets. Soon Blackler's Department Store and many smaller shops in Deane Street and Great Charlotte Street were on fire. Blackler's was badly damaged, with all the goods inside lost.

Two images of Liverpool City Centre taken in the immediate aftermath of an air raid. Had any significant time passed, some cleanup work would have been done, and the properties would normally be roped or fenced off whilst temporary repairs (known as first aid repairs) were undertaken. The first image on the left shows Parker Street, with Church Street in the background. The nearest property was badly damaged, with all of its windows and doors blown out, however it must have escaped serious structural damage as it remains standing today. In the background one of the city's trams runs along Church Street. It would be interesting to find out whether the clock had stopped at the time the building was damaged, or whether the wartime image was taken at 2:45pm the next day. No exact date was given for the photograph, however Parker Street was hit several times in the Blitz.

Meanwhile the Cook Street Arcade (seen here from Castle Street) was left in an even worse state after being hit during the May Blitz, and had to be demolished shortly afterwards, leaving only the external walls. The site was later used for an Emergency Water Supply.

The city's oldest building, the Bluecoat Chambers in School Lane came under threat when fires started in nearby premises. Like all large buildings, it contained its own fire watch party however the task was too great for them. The work of the Civil Defences was not helped by the fact that in many areas of the city, the water supply had failed, possibly due to broken mains caused by the bombing. The blaze soon caught hold and the east wing and much of the central block of the building were lost to the flames, although many important works of art were saved.

Taken from the Courtyard of the Bluecoat, this image demonstrates the damage done to the School Lane/Church Street junction during the raids. The building to the right of centre is only visible because the intervening property was destroyed in the blitz. This space is now taken up by Spinney House and is occupied by a clothing store.

As can be seen here, the East Wing of The Bluecoat (then known as Bluecoat Chambers) was badly damaged in the May Blitz. The survival of the city centre's oldest building was particularly fortunate given the difficulties faced by the civil defence units nearby.

The view from College Lane towards Seel Street with Hanover Street running past. It was not far from this junction that the Littlewoods Factory, mentioned on page 109, stood.

A view down Seel Street towards the junction in the photograph above. The area covered by these two images was badly bombed in the May Blitz.

The damage to the central block of The Bluecoat can be clearly seen in this photograph. The tanks filled with water in the foreground were part of a scheme to protect nearby buildings from the kind of fire damage which afflicted the building behind. It was one of many types of emergency water supply developed.

The Head Post Office of Liverpool occupied a large site between Whitechapel and Victoria Street and had already been hit at least once during the air raids (during the March Blitz) but had managed to remain in operation. According to John Hughes' excellent account of the May Blitz, *A Port in a Storm*, the building was well-defended, but suffered because the roof was undergoing repairs. This meant that there was tarpaulin covering the holes, and timber nearby waiting to be used.

Such a large building proved all but impossible to defend successfully once the flames caught hold. Initially, the efforts were made by the building's own fire watch party and the Home Guard detachment and staff, but they could only do so much, especially as more bombs followed shortly afterwards. Following an urgent request, the AFS sent as many appliances as they could, with some coming from as far afield as Allerton (a demonstration of how important the authorities considered the building to be). They soon found that they were fighting a losing battle. At one stage, the struggle to save the building became even harder when the flames caught up with some small arms ammunition stored in the building, setting it off. The addition of what may have sounded like a gun battle to the hellish scene would not have made the operation any easier!

The defenders retreated slowly through the building, saving as much of the post and valuables as they could. At around 4.00 am, the steel girders in the roof of the stores collapsed, but by then the defenders had been pulled out by the superintendent in charge of the operation. The result of the heroic efforts of those present was that although the building was

Modern day buses pass the badly damaged Head Post Office. This view looks from the junction of Sir Thomas Street and Victoria Street. The upper floors of the building were removed at a later date.

Another view of the Head Post Office, probably taken a little later than the one above as more scaffolding has been erected on the building, confirming that extensive repair work is being undertaken. This view is from Victoria Street and looks towards the junction above.

Government Buildings, damaged in the May Blitz, were demolished after the raids. At the time of writing plans have been put forward to develop the site into a multistorey car park, replacing the current open plan car park.

effectively rendered out of action, most of the post, the vital equipment and records survived. For the immediate future, operations were transferred to the Fruit Exchange whilst repairs were undertaken to the ground floor of the Post Office building.

Government Buildings, which stood diagonally opposite the Head Post Office was also struck by bombs. This large building had an important role to play in the administration of the area as it contained the Ministries of Health and Agriculture, the Inland Revenue Stamp Office and the Assistance Board. Not much is docuemmted about the events here, however it is known that a high explosive struck the building, crashing through the upper floors and doing severe damage to a basement which was sheltering a group of fire watchers.

Several were trapped and were only able to escape thanks to the efforts of one of their number, Ernest Leatham, who managed to free himself and find help. He summoned AFS support to deal with the fires blazing through the building, and a nearby police constable to help dig people out.

Leatham remained on the site for around seven hours despite the obvious danger and was later awarded the BEM (British Empire Medal) for his efforts.

On Hanover Street, the Littlewoods factory was struck by a high explosive just before midnight, completely destroying the building and killing three fire watchers who were present, but thanks to the foresight of Cecil Moores (see previous day) none of the normal night shift was hurt.

Left: The overhead railway was particularly vulnerable to enemy action as it lay close to the docks. The track bed was severed several times during the blitz, but always put back into operation shortly afterwards, due to its important role in transporting people along the length of the dock system. This image is from the Pierhead area, with a modern bus passing by, its passengers probably oblivious to the damage of yesteryear.

Below: Properties on Brunswick Street between Fenwick Street and the Strand were particularly badly hit in the May Blitz as this image shows. India Buildings (the tall building to the left of centre) survived despite a serious fire.

James Street station was damaged during the raid on 3/4 May 1941. The tall tower once contained the hydraulic water system that powered the lifts mentioned below.

Although few details are known, several sources state that the Custom House was hit on this night. Already damaged earlier in the raids, the May Blitz would inflict a fatal blow to this once grand building.

Most of James Street was devastated by both incendiaries and high explosives, leaving a chaotic situation, particularly at the station midway along the street. Rubble from the collapse of nearby warehouses that had been set alight crashed through the rear windows of the station building. This was soon gutted by the fire, which threatened to spread further.

As the station platforms were all underground, many people would use these as an unofficial shelter in much the same way as Londoners used the Underground. On this particular night though, they were cut off from any possible exit by the fires above. The station used a hydraulic lift system which was put out of action by the flames. A second exit onto Water Street was also blocked by falling debris near India Buildings.

Across the city centre at Central Station, the refreshment rooms were badly damaged by debris from Lewis's. The damage to one wall was so bad that the station itself was closed for a time.

India buildings on Water Street was not hit by bombs, but was surrounded on most sides by destruction or fires, with some of the latter eventually spreading to the building. With the fire services stretched to the full, and the fires spreading across all floors, it was a struggle to even keep the blaze from spreading further. It is a testament to the solid and modern construction methods used that it survived being burnt out without significant structural damage.

One incident, in particular, had a major impact on Liverpool's response to the raids. The telephone exchange on South John Street was burnt out, forcing its evacuation. The exchange controlled over 20,000 telephone lines, covering most of the city centre. In this age of mobiles and the internet, it is hard to imagine just what an impact this would have had. The civil defences did have alternative communication plans, including the use of messengers, but these all involved a delay in reaction times and made coordination of the already stretched defences even harder.

Also badly hit on this terrible night were most of the buildings on William Brown Street, including the Technical College, Picton Library, museum, the William Brown Library and Walker Art Gallery. A bomb landed behind the gallery, blasting out most of the windows nearby, whilst three incendiaries landed on the museum.

Church House, on the corner of South John Street and Lord Street, was also badly damaged in the May Blitz. The telephone exchange stood a little further down South John Street on the right in what is now the Liverpool One Shopping Centre.

The William Brown Library was hit by another device, which started a fire and trapped several people in the wreckage. Despite the fire spreading quickly, rescue workers managed to free the injured and move them to hospital. Help was also requested and received with dealing with the blaze, but both the William Brown Library and the nearby museum were badly damaged.

Over in Hatton Garden, the Salvage Corps headquarters was badly damaged when a high explosive bomb landed on the control room. Six people were killed nearby. The experience of many of the salvage men and their families on this night was particularly harrowing, as they were forced to abandon their shelter in the basement of the building and move to one under the Tramway offices nearby. They were then given no choice but to leave this as well due to the danger of a nearby fire. Most took shelter in the basement of a fire station opposite, but it is worth recalling that they would have had to take flight as the bombs were still falling and exploding nearby. Such an incredible odyssey is hard to imagine now, but through such desperate measures people were able to stay alive and find safety.

View towards Tithebarn Street and the damage inflicted during the raids. The two roads on the right are first Marybone and then Vauxhall Road, whilst Hatton Garden is the road on the left. It was further down the latter, that six people lost their lives when a high explosive hit the Salvage Corps control room.

The premises of the Peerless Refining Company seen from Cunliffe Street after the damage inflicted on it during the night of 3/4 May 1941. Palm oil from here was said to have ran down to Dale Street where it congealed.

The North Dispensary on Vauxhall Road after it was badly damaged in the May Blitz. The photograph was one of a series taken in November 1941 and shows the view from near the junction with Phillips Street. The exact date the building was damaged is unclear, but given the heavy damage to properties nearby, it was quite possibly the night of 3/4 May 1941. The building on the left is the former Marble Hall Hotel which is now a cafe.

Much of the area immediately north of the city centre, particularly around Vauxhall Road, Naylor Street and Marybone, which contained a lot of factories and warehouses, was heavily damaged. The loss of these buildings was a double blow as they often contained valuable goods and raw materials, many of them crucial to the war effort.

Also particularly badly hit were Wolstenholme Square, the Leyton Paper Mills on Henry Street, the Tatler Cinema and the magistrates court. Large fires caused damage at Princes Dock, Riverside Station, Duke's Dock, Canning Dock, Salthouse Dock, East Wapping Basin, Stewarts' warehouse in Gower Street and on the SS *Clan McInnes* in North King's number 2 Dock. The SS *Malakand,* an ammunition ship in Huskisson Dock caught fire and exploded the next morning, devastating the surrounding area.

An ammunition train was also set on fire at Breck Road Railway siding, resulting in extensive damage to property. Sudley Road Council School, Rose Lane Council School, Waterloo Dock and the Corporation yard on Smithdown Road were all seriously damaged during the raid. The Fountains Road area was devastated, with around a hundred people killed. Other badly hit residential areas included Creswick Street, Northumberland Terrace, Venmore Street, Towson Street and Hermia Street. St Mary's in Walton was also burnt out by a fire started by an incendiary.

This branch of Martins Bank, which stood on the corner of Smithdown Road and Langdale Road was badly damaged during the raid on 3/4 May 1941. Four people lost their lives in this area during the raid.

Anfield Road School and Leyfield School both suffered extensive damage. The Mill Road Hospital was devastated by a mine which exploded between C and E blocks, demolishing both and damaging others. Around eighty people were killed, but the prompt reaction of the rescue squads in freeing those trapped, and the ambulance service in transferring patients to other hospitals kept this total lower than it might otherwise have been.

An underground shelter, known as 'The Rocket' at the junction of Broad Green Road and Edge Lane Drive was hit and nearly thirty people were killed.

Daylight brought relief from the bombs, but everyone could tell that the raid had been severe. Large fires still raged across the city, despite the heroic efforts of the fire fighters, and many thousands were homeless. Many would leave the city, or attempt to before the end of the week, trying to find safety in nearby towns or the countryside. Most people would stay though, determined to make a stand and defend their city against the raiders.

Moving onto Bootle, the borough was also subjected to a devastating raid. Incendiaries started fires in houses in Akenside Street, Bulwer Street, Peel Road, Boswell Street, Bibby's Lane, Stuart Road and Melville Road.

Although described in the reports as being destroyed, at least the facade of the Cunard Furnishing Stores in Marsh Lane, Bootle survived the raids and still provides the frontage for the modern premises.

The remains of Scotts Bakery on Knowsley Road in Bootle, after it had been bombed during the night of 3/4 May 1941.

Other buildings to suffer damage from incendiaries include the General Post Office building, Williams Toffee Factory, Scott's Bakery on Knowsley Road, the Rates Office of the Borough Treasurer's Department, a timber yard in Well Lane, Johnsons Dyeworks, a warehouse in Bedford Place, a varnish works in Litherland Road, the Girls' Secondary School in Breeze Hill and St Monica's Church. The Cunard Furnishing Store in Marsh Lane was effectively destroyed.

High explosives were also scattered across the borough, with thirty-two landing between the docks and Stanley Road and another nine being reported between Stanley Road and Watts Lane.

Other areas damaged included Coleridge Street, Seaview Road, Tennyson Street, Southey Street, where over twenty houses were demolished, Shelley Street, Bibby's Lane, Goldsmith Street, Hemans Street, Longfellow Street, Somerset Road, Worcester Road, Southport Road, Hatfield Road, Connolly Avenue, Williams Avenue, Myerscough Avenue and the junction of Litherland Road and Marsh Lane.

Houses in Somerset Road, Bootle, damaged during the night of 3/4 May 1941 and later replaced with garages.

A picture of numbers 141 to 145 Southport Road, which were repaired or rebuilt after bomb damage. The photograph dates from the December raids, but similar damage was done during the May raids as well.

The Vernons Pools building in Linacre Lane was damaged, whilst some unexploded bombs were also reported in Oriel Road (opposite the Town Hall) and Hawthorne Road. Both were reported as being safely dealt with by the bomb disposal squads.

Perhaps the most tragic incident in the borough that night though occurred at the St Andrew's Church Hall at about midnight. The hall was sheltering people who had been made homeless by the raids, along with volunteer staff who were manning the rest centre. A high explosive struck the hall, demolishing it and killing thirty-seven people, five of whom were volunteer staff from the WVS (Women's Voluntary Service). An unknown number of people had left the rest centre earlier that evening to take shelter in the countryside, believing that to be a safer option.

The incident prompted the authorities to issue tighter guidelines, stating that people in rest centres should remain in shelters during the alerts and only return to the centre when the all clear sounded. Unfortunately, for the victims of the St Andrew's Church Hall bombing, this warning came too late.

The shattered remains of St Andrew's Church hall in Bootle after it was demolished on the night of 3/4 May 1941. The church itself is just out of shot on the right.

Above: View of houses on the corner of Litherland Road (running from left to right) and Marsh Lane that were demolished during the raid on 3/4 May 1941. Two people were killed in this area as a result of the raid, a father and daughter who lived at number 305. The Gas Works is a short way up Marsh Lane on the right, close to the bridge over the Leeds Liverpool Canal.

Left: This shows the heavily damaged facade of Johnsons Dye Works on Mildmay Road, Bootle after the May Blitz. According to the incident reports, the building was effectively burnt out during the raids, although this probably refers to only part of the company's premises, since the building in the distance still looks like it is in good condition. The view here looks from the junction with Stanley Road, towards Hornby Boulevard in the distance.

Churches and houses destroyed by the raids on Bootle on 3/4 May 1941. Above is the Welsh Presbyterian Church on the corner of Trinity Road and Stanley Road.

Right shows the damage to numbers 54-58 Cowper Street. None of these survived to the modern day, although a new church was built after the war.

Two more images of the damage inflicted on Bootle during the May Blitz. The first above is of the engineering premises of Edward Wilson and Son on Aintree Road. The second shows the properties which once stood on Hawthorne Road in Bootle, near the junction with Linacre Road.

The latter were still standing until a few years ago, but the site has now been developed into housing of the type seen on the left here. Both of these were originally undated, however recent research has revealed that the damage occurred at the height of the May Blitz, the night of 3/4 May 1941.

Damage done to the original entrance to Bootle's Marsh Lane and Strand Road Station (now called Bootle New Strand) during the May Blitz. Although no specific date was given on the photograph, the station is known to have been hit during the night of 3/4 May 1941. Of particular note are the wartime posters underneath the bridge, which advertise Mackeson Stout, Persil Washing Powder and the Hearts of Oak Benefit Society.

The nearest poster is part of a government propaganda campaign, encouraging ship builders to 'Speed the Ships'. Although not visible here due to the poster being damaged, it would also have said 'Every Rivet a Bullet'. Part of a campaign to keep morale on the home front high, it aimed to persuade those working in factories that their efforts were every bit as important as those in the armed forces or Merchant Navy, both of which after all needed as many ships as they could get given the losses in the Battle of the Atlantic at this stage of the war.

The burnt out shell of Waterloo Public Library and Museum on Prince Street, Crosby. The building was gutted by fires started by incendiaries which fell here on the night of 3/4 May 1941. The library site is now a car park.

In common with its neighbours to the south, Crosby was also badly hit. High explosives fell on Morningside, Brooklands Avenue, Buttermere Gardens, Balliol Grove, Tudor Road, Warren Road, Elm Road, Liverpool Road, Church Road, Nicholas Road, the Serpentine, St Mary's Road, and Sandy Road, the shore near Fort Crosby, Little Crosby Road and farm land near Brook Road.

Parachute mines landed on Bedford Place, Warburton Road and on land north of Hall Road East. It is impossible to say how many incendiary bombs were dropped, but Waterloo Public Library and Museum and the premises of Halls Furniture Store on South Road were hit. Across the borough, a total of twenty-four people were killed and fifty-one injured were injured. Twenty-four houses were demolished, 115 badly damaged, and over a thousand slightly damaged.

Two views of the gutted remains of Halls Furniture Removals on South Road, Waterloo.

The damage was done by incendiaries which landed on the night of 3/4 May 1941.

Houses in Balliol Grove, Crosby were hit by high explosives during the night of 3/4 May 1941. Nobody was killed, despite the heavy damage. However in Trinity Grove, another close off Riverslea Road, four people were killed. No photograph of that incident appears to have been taken, or if it was, it has not survived.

The wartime photograph used here is from Beryl Road in Prenton and was originally thought to show number 30, however closer study of the gates in the wartime photograph reveals that the drive and gates actually belonged to number 32, making this the correct comparison. The property on the left, which was also damaged in the raid, is number 34. The damage was done during the early days of the May Blitz.

The May Blitz had a limited impact on the Wirral. Although householders would naturally prefer that their road not be bombed at all, the owners of these houses in Carlaw Road could count themselves lucky in that the only damage appears to have been to the outer walls and gateposts of their properties. The exact date of these photographs (and that of Beryl Road on the previous page) is unknown, other than it was during May 1941.

The residents of these houses in Heath Drive in Upton had little to be thankful for, though. An unexploded bomb smashed into number 36, eventually destroying the property, but strangely leaving the outer walls and gates intact, suggesting the bomb landed to the rear of the house or directly on it. The man walking in front of the blitzed property is believed to be a postman. According to one account cited in *Birkenhead at War* the destruction was caused by an unexploded bomb which fell on 1/2 May 1941 and exploded some time later before it could be defused.

In Wallasey, medium-sized high explosives were scattered across the borough, landing in Rake Lane, Laburnum Road, Cliff Road, Belvidere Road, Kent Road, Breck Road, Burnside Road, Princess Road, Wallasey Road, Leander Road, Colville Road, and Stourcliffe Road. They also damaged properties in Hazeldene Avenue, Oakdale Avenue, Parry Street Mostyn Street and Courtney Avenue.

Elsewhere on the Wirral, bombs landed in fields in Bromborough doing limited damage to overhead wires. Other high explosives landed in Thornton Hough, where no damage seems to have been done and in Higher Bebington where four shops were affected.

This civil defence worker is studying the terrible damage inflicted on what was once the premises of Austin Reed, a firm of tailors based in St George's Crescent, Liverpool. The building and most of the surrounding area was severely damaged in the May Blitz and had to be rebuilt after the war in a modern style. The road to the right of Austin Reed's property is Lord Street.

This property on the corner of Wallasey Road (left) and Belvidere Road (right) was also demolished in the May Blitz. It was replaced by an almost identical building on the same spot, leaving behind no trace of the damage being inspected here, but this at least kept the row of buildings intact.

4/5 MAY 1941

The Luftwaffe continued to pound the region remorselessly. The fact that the raid was lighter than the previous night's would have been slight consolation to people who were still dealing with the massive damage and fires. Probably the biggest casualty of the raid was a property in Great George Square which was being used as a boarding house for seamen. More than twenty of them, mostly Belgians, lost their lives when the building was hit by a high explosive bomb.

Bombs also demolished houses in Catherine Street, Mountjoy Street, Magnum Street and Bingley Road. A clinic in Northumberland Street was hit, as was a gas holder in Athol Street and also Sandhills Station and St Sylvester's School. The Rotunda Theatre was destroyed by fire (fuelled by the fact it was being used to store furniture from bombed houses) and a parachute mine seriously damaged Walton Lane School. In Aintree, the Union Cold Storage premises were severely damaged.

Although the wartime photograph is undated, one likely victim of the raid on the night of 4/5 May 1941 was number 11 Nelson Street, Liverpool. The building stood near the corner of Nelson Street and Great George Square. It was not far from here that more than twenty seamen (many of them Belgians) lost their lives on that night. Belgium had been overrun by Nazi Germany the previous year, and servicemen from many of these occupied countries served gallantly in British army, navy and air force units.

The view down Brunswick Street from the junction with Lower Castle Street. The rubble immediately behind the cars is all that remains of the Corn Exchange, whilst in the distance the remains of various badly damaged buildings can be made out. This area suffered a great deal during the May Blitz, but we can be grateful that so many architectural gems survived, even whilst others were lost forever.

The view up Brunswick Street towards Castle Street in the distance reveals more of the damage done in this area during the May Blitz. This time the Corn Exchange is on the right, with the former branch of the Bank of England in the distance (also seen on page 104). The imposing bulk of the India Buildings, which were burnt out in the May Blitz but still survived, is on the left.

A close study of the photograph reveals that the junction with Fenwick Street has been blocked off to traffic, a common post air raid measure, when an area was considered to still be dangerous.

Meanwhile the photograph on the right shows more of the heavy damage done to the Lord Street/ Paradise Street area. Most of the business premises on these two streets were destroyed or badly damaged. Also of note, is the sign to the right of centre, diverting traffic to the left. This would be impossible now as this area is a pedestrian only zone. The building on the left was once occupied by the firm of Coopers, a well known and much loved department store.

Another probable victim of the May Blitz were these houses which stood on the corner of Hardy and Grenville Streets in the south of the city. In the background, is the imposing bulk of the Anglican Cathedral which dominates this area.

The civil defence worker in this photograph is standing near the two houses on Hawthorne Road mentioned on the next page. Neither of these buildings is still standing today.

In Bootle, the night brought several bombs. One that landed at the corner of Strand Road and Stanley road damaged ten houses, whereas another that fell at the junction of Hawthorne Road and Park Street, badly damaged two.

At the corner of Oxford Road and Hawthorne Road, a house and a wholesale fruit and vegetable warehouse were hit and set on fire. Clare Road and the nearby part of Southport Road were also struck. St John's School in Brasenose Road was damaged, as were twenty-four houses in Brasenose Road and Bedford Place. Bianca Street saw two houses badly hit with others damaged. Several houses in Orlando Street were also affected.

Crosby suffered less, although several bombs still fell on the borough during the night, all of them were high explosives. These landed on Schubert Street, Seaforth Road, Beaumaris Street and the Greyhound Track on Crosby Road South. Nineteen people were injured, two houses badly damaged and around a hundred were slightly damaged, but fortunately, nobody was killed.

In Wallasey, three people were killed when a parachute mine went off in Burnside Avenue – these were the borough's only fatalities during the May Blitz. Damage was also done to Rosebery Avenue, Fender Lane, Burdens Field, Tiverton Avenue, The Mount, Manor Lane, Wellington Road and the grounds of the Grammar School.

This shows the heavy damage that was done to the corner of Mostyn Street and Burnside Road, Wallasey, on the night of 4/5 May 1941. Although the house on the corner of the two has been flattened, most of the surrounding property has suffered only fairly light damage, and nobody was killed in either street.

5/6 MAY 1941

More raiders passed overhead and some very iconic buildings were lost or damaged. Serious damage was done by high explosives to St Nicholas' Church, the parish church of Liverpool and one familiar to most of its residents. Already blitzed in the December raids, it was burnt out completely after this raid, leaving only the tower intact.

Warehouses in Lancelot's Hey, the Salvation Army Hostel in Park Lane, South Castle Street, the Bluecoat Building, Duke's Grain Warehouse, West King's Dock Quay and South Canning Dock, a chemical works on Hardy Street, the Great George Street Congregational Church, the gas office on Duke Street, St Luke's Church on Leece Street, St Luke's School on Colquitt Street, number 2 ward of the Royal Infirmary, a nurses' home on Mulberry Street, St Silas' Church on Pembroke Place, and the T J Hughes store on London Road were all hit near the city centre.

Further afield, serious damage was done to tenements on Northumberland Street, as well as houses in the Lodge Lane Area and a dining room on Coburg Dock Avenue. A public house on Christian Street was demolished, houses on Harvey Street and Smithdown Road, and flour mills on Glasgow Street were also seriously damaged, whilst several corporation tenement blocks were struck.

Damage done to the top end of Bold Street, Liverpool believed to have been done during the May Blitz, most likely during the night of 5/6 May 1941, when most of this area was hammered. The building in the centre was a branch of the Liverpool Savings Bank at the time, whilst the one on the right is all that remains of a branch of Barclays Bank.

One particularly unlucky firm during the May Blitz was Grayson Rollo and Clover Ltd, a ship repair and engineering firm with several sites across Merseyside. Two in particular were badly hit during that dark week, the first, shown on the right, stood in Bridgewater Street near the South Docks. The second, shown below, stood at the junction of Sandhills Lane and Bankhall Road, not far from Sandshill Station.

Although unfortunate, it was not particularly surprising that the firm's buildings suffered damage during the raids. The premises were spread out, but usually close to the river and docks due to the nature of their work, which placed them in the firing line.

Not all bombing incidents were total disasters as these images show. It would have unquestionably been a major inconvenience for the residents of these homes, but compared to some of the damage being done at this time, they would probably have counted themselves lucky.

The photograph above shows damage to number 13 Bessborough Road, whilst that on the left shows damage to houses on either side of number 425 Woodchurch Road, Prenton. Both date from the night of 5/6 May 1941.

Fires across the city were described as being extensive, with the worst being in the Duke Street and Renshaw Street areas. Many salt water mains, connected straight to the sea were utilized. There was also a slight fire at the cathedral, whilst a large area around Bold Street and Colquitt Street was alight.

Remarkably, Bootle escaped the night unscathed, despite the raiders hitting targets everywhere else in the region. In Crosby, one high explosive landed in fields, but nobody was killed or injured.

After a comparatively quiet couple of nights, bombs fell on Birkenhead again, hitting Bessborough Road, Cranbourne Avenue, Northwood Road, Carlaw Road, Ingestre Road and Ingleborough Road.

In Bebington, they fell on the Woodhey area, whilst Wallasey was hit by bombs in Mill Lane, Vale Park, Holland Road, Ashburton Road and Hartington Road. A number also fell on open countryside in the Moreton area. Further afield on the Wirral, ten bombs landed near Arrowe Brook Farm doing no damage, whilst nine landed near Neston, with little impact.

Damage to the Waterworks cottages on Prenton Hall Road, Prenton.

A stark and grim reminder of the Luftwaffe's ability to transform lives comes in the form of this small child, standing in front of the shattered remains of 52-54 Northwood Road, Prenton. Her identity is unknown, as is whether she had any connection to the houses.

All of these properties were damaged during the raid on the night of 5/6 May 1941.

6/7 MAY 1941

The night brought no respite, with the raid lasting over four hours. In Liverpool, high explosives damaged the Parcel Post Office in Hatton Garden, the Landing Stage (where passengers boarded ferries) and the Ferry Goods Stage. Serious fires started at the Custom House and Bents Brewery in Johnson Street. The Town Hall suffered a near miss, but had most of its windows broken and damage was done to the Council Chamber.

High explosives also demolished several houses in the Kensington district, whilst St Catherine's Church in Abercromby Square was gutted by fire. Mill Street Police Station was blighted by incendiaries and a serious fire caused damage to Wilson's Flour Mills in Mill Street. In the South Docks, damage was done to East Harrington Shed, West Harrington Shed, two sides of the Albert Dock, South Coburg Shed, the service pipe line at Dingle Jetty and a police hut at North East Brunswick Dock. High explosives landed on the Brunswick Gardens tenements and Cheshire Lines Committee Goods Station.

The damaged premises of the Liverpool and London and Globe Insurance Company on the corner of High Street and Dale Street in Liverpool City Centre. The building was hit by the same devices which knocked about the Town Hall (just out of shot to the left) on the night of 6/7 May 1941.

This picture shows houses in Hillside Road, Tranmere after they were heavily damaged in the raid of 6/7 May 1941. The properties, numbered 57-61 have since been replaced with modern housing. Also hit on the same night, was Hillside Road School, which was a little further up the road, and Williams Yard, a little further down.

North of the city centre, high explosives struck the overhead railway causing heavy damage. Ships in Bramley Moore Dock were seriously damaged and two barges in South Stanley Dock were sunk. An engineering works in Charters Street was gutted by fire.

Some houses in Liverpool were damaged by faulty anti-aircraft shells which exploded on impact. This type of 'friendly fire' was unfortunately relatively common. Neither Bootle nor Crosby suffered any damage in this raid.

In Birkenhead, bombs fell in the town centre, on Cleveland Street, Douglas Street, Duncan Street, John Street; plus the Woodside Hotel, Leicester Street, Poulton Bridge, Station Road (by Birkenhead North Station) and Taylor Street.

In Tranmere, they fell on Caerwys Grove, Clovers Shipyard, Cranbrooke Avenue, Hillside Road, St Catherine's School, Holborn Hill, Holt Hill, Queen's Place, Quigley Street and Seymour Street. Meanwhile, in Bebington, high explosives and incendiaries landed in Rock Park.

7/8 May 1941

The raiders pounded the region remorselessly, although unusually, on this occasion, very little damage was done to the city centre. However, overall, it was probably the second worst night of the May Blitz, and its impact was severe as most of the bombs fell in just two hours.

A workshop on Pembroke Place and builder's yard on Fairclough Lane were gutted by fire and serious blazes also broke out at a cooperage in Gildarts Gardens and a stables in Dickson Street. In the city centre, a bomb struck Tower Buildings, falling down a lift shaft and injuring four people when it blew up an air raid shelter. Another also demolished the Shakespeare Hotel in Whitechapel, burying several people.

Parachute mines fell on Sandholme Street and Teulon Street, destroying houses and three air raid shelters. This whole area saw widespread damage, with houses, schools and churches destroyed. The Stanley Road Bridge over the railway was smashed, whilst rolling stock at Bankhall Carriage Sidings was destroyed. A warehouse in Townsend Street was demolished, and damage was done to the Sandon Motor Works on Grundy Street.

One of many photographs taken after the May Blitz in the area of the Strand, this looks towards the Goree Warehouses, behind which would be Tower Buildings mentioned above.

Surface shelters were demolished in Beatrice Street and Norris Street. An AFS pump and a Lancashire County Police mobile canteen were destroyed. Many houses in the Scotland Road area were hit. Walton Gaol lost E block when it was blitzed by a large explosive, adding to the damage done earlier in the week, forcing the authorities to transfer prisoners elsewhere until repairs could be done. Nearby Walton Hospital was also hit, as was Walton Junction Station.

The AFS station in Forth Street was damaged, as was Lambeth Road School, and a distillery on Juniper Street, a shelter on Townsend Street, the British and American Tobacco Factory on Commercial Road and Carnarvon Road. Serious damage was also inflicted on the North Docks and railway sheds with three ships sinking. A parachute mine landed on Daffodil Road, causing serious damage to houses in the vicinity.

Having been fortunate enough to escape damage for two night's running, Bootle suffered badly in this raid. The devastation was so widespread that a full list of the roads affected would be impossible to include in this volume, so what follows is a snapshot of some of the worst incidents of the night.

Incendiaries were scattered across the borough and did considerable damage to both commercial *and* residential properties. Ordinarily, damage to houses was limited as the residents were present to put out the fires. The length and extent of the May raids however meant that most people spent the night in shelters, leaving their homes unattended.

One of the victims of these fire bombs was the Marsh Lane Baths, which was being used as a temporary mortuary. The bombs set the building on fire, incinerating the corpses in a makeshift crematorium. Of the 180 bodies present around forty had yet to be identified, and sadly thanks to the flames, they never would be.

Linacre Hospital was hit, with the bomb falling on number 7 pavilion, in use at the time as an ARP first aid post. This was demolished, with other pavilions being damaged too. At the time, they housed the Bootle General Hospital, which had moved from Derby Road due to its proximity to the docks.

The ARP Headquarters building on Knowsley Road suffered a direct hit, demolishing the main stores. This destroyed the borough's supply of gas masks, anti-gas equipment and clothing, but these were promptly replenished from central government. The anti-gas Cleansing Station and Rescue Service Depot were also badly damaged, whilst another bomb demolished the nearby Broadway Cinema and damaged a billiard hall.

By far the worst single incident of the night though was when bombs blew out a wall of the Co-Operative store on Stanley Road, collapsing the basement roof onto those sheltering below. This had been converted into an air raid shelter earlier in the war. At least thirty-six people died, with many escaping through the emergency hatches, or along tunnels to the nearby shops.

In Crosby, more than thirty high explosives, six parachute mines and an uncountable number of incendiaries struck the borough. Damage was widespread, with twenty-two people killed, fifty-six injured, nine houses demolished, forty badly, and over 200 slightly so. The most serious incidents were at Rawson Road, where a parachute mine exploded killing eight people, and also at Seaforth Vale, where a shelter was hit by a high explosive and at Hornby Street.

The impact was lessened by the fact that five of the six mines landed on the shoreline near Harbord Road, doing little or no damage. Had these landed in the midst of a residential area, the loss of life would have been much greater. It wasn't uncommon for high explosives to fall in fields or on the shoreline, doing little material damage.

These buildings at the corner of Strand Road and Stanley Road, Bootle were hit during the May blitz. The Co-Op shelter was located on the far side of the tall building on the left of the wartime image. Apart from a small row to the right of the theatre, none of these wartime buildings survive now.

The raid also saw bombs dropped on Wallasey, causing damage to Rolleston Drive, Lyndhurst Road, Victoria Road, Rowson Street, King's Parade, Tollemache Street, Grosvenor Road, Little Hope Street, Windsor Street and the rear of Waterloo Road. The ferry steamer *Royal Daffodil* also sank at her moorings at the Seacombe Landing Stage and would remain there for some time.

In Bromborough, two high explosives landed near Pool Lane, inflicting damage on houses and an adjacent maternity home. Rock Road was also hit, as were the premises of Fawcett Preston and Co.

8/9 MAY 1941

The last act of the May Blitz occurred with two parachute mines landing on Bootle. One fell on the gas works in Litherland Road and the other at the corner of Linacre Lane and Alt Road. The latter demolished eleven houses and caused damage to Linacre School. Some houses in nearby Lunt Road and Litherland Road were also affected. The impact of the first mine was quite considerable as it limited the production of gas for the town's supply.

The impact of the air raids on Liverpool's main shopping area was quite considerable. Church Street came through the raids marginally better than most others, but still lost several prominent buildings. The gap to the left of centre is where the buildings seen on page 46 once stood, lost in the raids of December 1940.

The junction to the right is Parker Street. Both Parker and Church Street, along with most of the city's shopping area is now pedestrianized. The tower of the former Coopers department store can be seen in the distance on the left, as can the twin towers of the Marks and Spencer store on the right. In the foreground on the left, is a sign for the YMCA, the Young Men's Christian Association. This group helped to feed troops during the war, and dealt with the huge numbers of refugees and displaced people.

Lord Street suffered badly, with most of the properties along it either destroyed or badly damaged. This view looks from near the Victoria Monument along Lord Street, with the blitzed remains of St George's Crescent on the right. Today's modern cars drive along the route followed by many wartime trams, the tracks for which are often still under the road surface.

This is another view of the St George's Crescent area, this time from Castle Street. This area was transformed by the construction of the Queen Elizabeth Law Courts (right background) in the 1970s. Prior to this, South Castle Street ran through that area. The Victoria Monument is just visible on the right.

Turning to the left from the above position would give you the following view along Harrington Street. Another victim of the May Blitz, much of the area has since been redeveloped. Both of these photographs were probably taken some time after the raids which caused the damage, as there has been time to clear the debris from the streets, and fence off the bomb sites to prevent people from gaining access to them.

LATE WAR RAIDS,
MAY 1941 – JANUARY 1942

With the May Blitz ending on 9 May 1941, the Luftwaffe's efforts against Merseyside and Britain in general began to tail off. The bomber squadrons were needed for other campaigns, such as those against the Balkans and Russia, with many being transferred east. Also British (and later, American) air attacks against Germany would draw enemy fighter squadrons back to the Third Reich to protect its cities against our own bombers.

For local people, it would have been difficult to judge when the raids ended, since the scattered nature of the attacks which followed the May Blitz left no guide either way. People could perhaps have been forgiven for returning to a relatively normal way of life, sleeping in their houses rather than in air raid shelters, and not rushing quite as fast to take cover when the sirens went off. This may seem complacent to us today, but it is worth remembering that a siren going off did not always mean the certainty of a raid. The Bootle authorities, for example, noted nearly thirty separate nights on which an alert was sounded between June and October 1941, but only on the last of these did any devices land in the Bootle area.

Although the raids were now few and far between, their impact could still be deadly. Two bombs fell on Bootle in a single night in October for example, but fifteen people were still killed and ninety-four were injured. People could not really afford to let their guard down as the Luftwaffe still had a sting in its tail.

One good thing to come from the bombing was that the many fire brigades were nationalized in August 1941 to create the National Fire Service (NFS). This made it quicker and simpler to deploy resources from one area to another.

Also emergency water supply sites began to spring up around the region, often on a bomb site that had been cleared. These took several forms, but were a reserve of water for use in fighting fires, helpful if the nearby mains were insufficient or damaged. Large shelters were also constructed at Tranmere and Bidston using a large tunnel system at each. Unfortunately although these shelters would have been very effective, they were only completed after the raids had finished, although there is some evidence of use before they officially opened. These efforts did at least demonstrate that the authorities were prepared to take additional steps to protect local people, recognizing the terrible experience that they had gone through.

The raids came to an end just 10 days into 1942, although the war in Europe would continue for more than three years. The Luftwaffe would continue to launch scattered raids against other cities, followed by the rocket attacks using V1s and V2s much later in the war. For Merseyside though, the blitz experience was finally over and the long hard work of rebuilding the region could start. In some areas, it could be argued that this process of restoration did not truly finish for decades. The legacy of the blitz endures to this day, long after the final bomber was seen in the skies.

In the aftermath of the May Blitz (often in November) a great many photographs were taken of the damage done to Liverpool. This image shows the remains of St Mary's Church on Highfield Street, just to the north of the City Centre and not far from the site of the former Exchange Station. Effectively destroyed in the raids, a new church would be built on the same site after the war. This too has been demolished in recent years, and the site remains empty today.

10/11 MAY 1941

Bombs from what was probably a lone raider fell on Green Lawn in Birkenhead. The damage appears to have been slight and nobody was killed.

28/29 MAY 1941

The reports of this night were somewhat contradictory. The police recalled damage to two areas, the Croxteth Hall Estate, where wheat fields caught fire, and the Beaumont Street area of Toxteth where eight houses were damaged. In both cases, the culprits were high explosives. However the records of the *Liverpool Daily Post & Echo* reporter Arthur Johnson (compiled by his son in *Merseyside's Secret Blitz Diary*) state that the damage was done by falling anti-aircraft shells. He also says this was much more widespread, with shells hitting Dove Street, Beaumont Street, Carrington Street and Granby Street in the Lodge Lane area, along with Normanby Street, Longmoor Lane and Utting Avenue elsewhere. It is quite likely that the

Just a short distance from St Mary's Church, the Tithebarn Street area was also badly damaged in the raids, with the section around the junction of Cheapside (right) particularly badly hit. This view looks towards the junction with Vauxhall Road/Marybone where the photograph on page 113 was taken.

damage was caused by a combination of falling anti-aircraft shells and bombs, since it would be unusual, although not unknown, for Liverpool to be ignored entirely on a night when both sides of the Mersey came under attack.

In Crosby, high explosives fell on 78-80 Moor Drive South, the rear gardens of 19-21 Moor Drive West, 12 The Byway, the Merchant Taylors' playing fields, in fields and in marshland to the rear of Carfield Cottages. Incendiaries landed on Moorland Avenue, Moor Lane, Poplar Avenue, Moor Drive South and Moor Drive West. One person was killed and two were injured. Four houses were badly damaged and eleven slightly damaged. Birkenhead was once again struck, with bombs falling on Beryl Road, Ford Road, Manor Drive, Manor Road and Rydal Avenue.

30/31 MAY 1941

Concentrating mostly on Liverpool's docks, this raid saw high explosives strike North Coburg Dock, North West Toxteth Dock, North East Brunswick Dock and the Coburg Grain Warehouse. Elsewhere in the city, bombs damaged services in Stanley Park Avenue and Pinehurst Avenue. Apart from this however, the damage appears to have been slight. In Birkenhead, bombs fell on Church Road (Upton), Houghton Road, Loretto Drive, Pool Lane and South Drive.

The original photograph of the Protestant Reformers Church is just recorded as being taken in May 1941 with no specific date. The damage was most likely done during the May Blitz, although it could possibly have been done later in the month. The church once stood on Netherfield Road South, between Conyers Street and Crete Street.

31 MAY/1 JUNE 1941

In Liverpool, during the early hours, incendiaries started small fires in the area around Gladstone Dock but had little impact. The high explosives which fell nearby had more of an effect, with naval stores damaged. Damage was also done to Alexandra and Hornby Docks, whilst high explosives fell in the County Road and Breeze Hill areas.

Bootle meanwhile recorded a light raid, with high explosives and incendiaries mostly being confined to the Oxford Road area. Three people were slightly injured, but otherwise damage was slight. Crosby bore the brunt of the raid, with nineteen high explosive bombs, two oil bombs, and four incidents of incendiaries. Such a high density of devices caused fourteen deaths, forty-eight injuries, destroyed twelve houses, badly damaged another dozen and slightly damaged around ninety.

In Wallasey, bombs fell on Bowden Road, Halton Road, Shelton Road, Seaview Road, Queensway, Sudworth Road, Gorsehill Road, the Big Yard in Wallasey Village, Inglewood Road, Cobham Road and Borrowdale Road.

Heswall suffered what was for the borough a large number of high explosives, the worst of which landed on a house in Village Road, killing three people and seriously injuring a fourth. Another landed on a cafe, trapping five people, whilst others fell on Telegraph Road and School Hill. No less than fourteen landed in fields, causing only very slight damage to nearby houses. Two oil bombs came down, one in a field near Davenport Road and another on the railway track near the station, causing slight damage to the track.

High Explosives which fell on the night of 31 May/1 June 1941 have damaged the side of this house in Queensway, Wallasey, exposing the staircase inside but leaving it mostly intact.

The former Laundry building on Grosvenor Road, Wallasey was badly damaged in the raid of 1/2 June 1941, with around half the building lost. The remainder would still be standing for many years, with a sweet shop on the near corner and a nightclub in the main part of the building for some time.

1/2 JUNE 1941

Wallasey appears to have been the main target on this night, with bombs falling on the St George's Park area, Grosvenor Drive and Grosvenor Road. In Rowson Street, Apperley's Garage caught fire, but swift action averted the potential danger to the petrol pumps. Bombs also fell in Hardie Avenue and Bermuda Road in Moreton and in Stringhey Road, Duke Street, St George's Mount and St James Road.

In Bromborough, a high explosive damaged houses and shops adjoining the police station, whilst another seriously damaged two houses in Great Sutton and slightly damaged another four.

24/25 JUNE 1941

After a gap of more than three weeks, the enemy raiders returned to the skies over Merseyside once more, although the scale of the raids was clearly diminishing as time passed. In Liverpool, two high explosives demolished part of a nursery in Macket's Lane, whilst another landed on locomotives in the North East Princes Dock, wreaking havoc. West Waterloo Dock also suffered damage, and a church in the Rose Hill area caught fire when incendiaries landed on it. There was also another case of 'friendly fire' as falling anti-aircraft shells damaged four partly assembled aeroplanes in Speke.

In Birkenhead, at least nine high explosive bombs landed on the borough. Roads hit included Cathcart Street, Cleveland Street, Corporation Road, Dock Road, Hilbre Street, Prenton Road West, Vittoria Street and Rendel Street. In Rock Ferry, bombs landed in Rock Park, Bedford Drive, Southdale Road, Westdale Road and Roxburgh Avenue. In Tranmere, they hit Allcott Avenue. Bombs also damaged the East Float grain warehouses and some nearby old dock warehouses.

Two views of the damage inflicted on the junction of Westdale and Southdale Road, Rock Ferry during the raid of 24/25 June 1941, a heavy one by late war standards. The above image looks from Westdale Road and shows the severe damage done to several houses on that side.

The image on the left shows that the house on the other side of Westdale Road suffered quite heavy damage to one corner, but for the most part, it remained intact. At least four people were killed on this night in the immediate vicinity and one other person was killed a little further down Southdale Road. Not far from the far end of Westdale Road stands the Well Lane Police station, whilst Victoria Park is at the far end of Southdale Road.

Relatively light damage inflicted on the properties on the corner of Magazine Lane (left) and Seabank Road (right). The date for this damage is hard to pin down as no date is given in the archives, however both roads are recorded as being hit during the raid on 1/2 June 1941, suggesting this date.

In Wallasey, Dalmorton Road, Vaughan Road, Gorsedale Road, Seabank Road, Magazine Lane, Kelvin Road, the Dock Road, Oakdale Road, Dalton Road and Westbank Avenue were all hit by high explosives of varying sizes. Two people were injured, one of them seriously.

Bebington did not escape damage either, as an area of pine woods along Storeton Ridge was hit, setting it alight. In Heswall, the Church of England school house and Telegraph Road were hit.

23/24 JULY 1941

Liverpool suffered no direct damage from enemy action, but falling anti-aircraft shells damaged houses in the north of the city, specifically in the Everton and County Road areas. The shells seem to have been fired by the local batteries at bombers over Birkenhead, since this was the only part of the region where bombs landed in significant numbers.

The worst incident of the night came at Arthur Street in Birkenhead, where a bomb demolished a street shelter, blowing out its walls and bringing the concrete roof down, killing eight people. Duke Street, Cavendish Street, Cleveland Street, Mollington Street, Frederick Street and Naylor Street were also damaged. In Tranmere, Olive Mount and Holt Hill were both struck. Elsewhere, bombs fell near the foreshore in Hoylake, and near the fort in Crosby, without causing significant damage at either spot.

27 SEPTEMBER 1941

Another example of damage without enemy action occurred at around 9.37 am, when a barrage balloon came down on the roof of numbers 20-24 Molyneux Road, Crosby. No damage is recorded for the incident but at the very least it must have been a major inconvenience.

12 OCTOBER 1941

In Crosby, a stick of four high explosive bombs landed near the Rimrose Brook. None of them exploded and they all came to earth in fields, although one fell just 70 yards from nearby Eden Drive. It is interesting to note that this incident occurred after the Borough Engineer and Surveyor (R Fothergill) had completed a large, handwritten book containing a thorough record of the bombs dropped on the borough, along with the dates, times and locations for

Numbers 21 and 23 Power Road, Rock Ferry, as seen from Woodward Road after their demolition by high explosives in the October 1941 raids, exposing the houses behind. Two people were killed in the area during that month.

each device. It would seem that having gone more than four months without any bombs falling; the authorities had thought the raids were all but over.

That small stick of bombs was in fact the last enemy action against Crosby.

20/21 OCTOBER 1941

After a short gap, the raiders returned to the skies over Merseyside once more. In Birkenhead town centre, bombs fell on Borough Road, Cathcart Street, Corporation Road, Mason Street and Vittoria Dock. In Noctorum, Beryl Road and Noctorum Avenue were hit, whilst in Rock Ferry, Alpha Drive and Power Road schools were struck.

Meanwhile, Bootle suffered its first raid in over four months. At least two large devices landed on the borough, with one falling in Surrey Street, where twenty houses were destroyed and sixty damaged. The other landed between Gloucester Road and Worcester Road, with eight houses demolished and forty-four damaged. Other roads affected by the blasts included Rutland Street, Brookhill Road, Suffolk Street, Hawthorne Road (the school there was damaged) Sussex Street, Litherland Road, Fernhill Road, Norfolk Street and Kent Street.

The close proximity of these locations, combined with the size of each blast, believed to be parachute mines on each occasion, caused great destruction in many nearby streets. The Corporation's ARP garage and the gas holders in Linacre Gas works were also damaged.

Casualties in Bootle amounted to fifteen people killed, sixty-five seriously injured and twenty-nine slightly hurt. Part of the reason for the high number of casualties, considering the low number of incidents, was that there had been several false alarms in recent months. Locals had become complacent, as they were used to sirens sounding, and began to wait for the sound of bombs falling nearby before they headed for the shelters. Since these two large devices were amongst the first dropped locally that night, there was no chance for many of those in the affected streets. This proved to be the final attack of the war against Bootle.

22/23 OCTOBER 1941

In Liverpool, the police reports state that although nobody was hurt in the raid, falling anti-aircraft shells did some damage in A and F Police Divisions. Presumably, the gunners were firing at the planes attacking Birkenhead and Bebington. The shells were recorded as falling on the National and Provincial Bank on Water Street, and they also hit Hale Road, Banks Road Recreation Ground, and Reynolds Park in Woolton.

In Birkenhead, bombs fell on Mason Street and Woodchurch Road. In Rock Ferry, they landed on Alpha Drive Schools, Highfield Road, Highfield South, New Chester Road, Ravenswood Avenue and Woodward Road. In Bebington, bombs fell on Broadway and the King's Park and Bebington Village areas. At least two houses were demolished and several badly damaged. Bebington Parish Church was also closed for a week due to an unexploded bomb landing in the Vicarage.

Further afield, an anti-aircraft shell fell on the garden of 14 Albert Road, West Kirby and exploded in the garden, sadly killing one person. Two high explosives also landed in the Eastham Rake area, damaging twenty houses and injuring one person. Four further high explosives landed in a field near Warren Farm in Eastham Woods, but only slightly damaged nearby properties.

1 NOVEMBER 1941

In this penultimate raid on Liverpool, remarkably little damage was done. High explosives landed on a cottage in woods on the Croxteth Estate, but other than that, the only damage was caused when an anti-aircraft shell fell on 27 Lomond Road.

This night saw the final raid on Birkenhead, with bombs falling on Cottage Street, Livingstone Street and Price Street. It was a bad time for Wallasey, with bombs falling in Prospect Vale, Beverley Road, Vyner Road, Studley Road, Sandy Lane and Broadway Avenue. Two people were killed in this final raid on the Wallasey area.

In Bebington, the night saw a high explosive bomb blow a huge crater in a garden behind Town Lane and Malpas Drive, but luckily nobody was killed. However, three residents at 146 Town Lane were killed when a bomb landed there. Elsewhere in the borough, bombs landed in Bebington Village, southern Bebington, Brackenwood, and Woodhey. In Port Sunlight, they hit Bolton Road and Pool Bank. Bombs also fell in Meols, Raby, Great Sutton and Hoylake.

Numbers 29 and 31 Vyner Road, Wallasey were flattened by high explosives during the final raid on the borough. Number 33 has also suffered some damage to the side wall of the property.

Further victims of Wallasey's final raid of the war were numbers 29 and 31 Beverley Road, seen here from Aysgarth Road. The damage has attracted the attention of a group of children, and quite a lot of men are already at work in the ruins of the buildings. They would either be checking to ensure there was nobody trapped in the rubble, or starting the long and exhausting process of clearing up in preparation for the site to be used again.

Despite the occasional enemy raid, life in the city had to go on, as the war was still raging and the region had a crucial role to play in keeping the country's supply routes open. Many of the dock warehouses had been hit during the raids, such as this one, which is attached to Stanley Dock. The far end of the building was damaged during the war, but this did not stop it from being patched up and kept in use. The barges in the dock would have come down the Leeds Liverpool Canal. The former warehouse is now back in use with a hotel using parts of both the old and new structure.

10/11 JANUARY 1942

The Luftwaffe paid another visit to the skies above Liverpool, dropping bombs on Stanhope Street, Berkley Street and Upper Stanhope Street, damaging or demolishing quite a large number of houses. Sadly, 15 people were killed in the raid.

One of those properties hit was 102 Upper Stanhope Street, which had ironically been the former home of Adolf Hitler's half-brother, Alois Hitler. Alois and his Irish-born wife had lived in the city for a few years. Some people have even suggested that Adolf visited his brother in Liverpool just before the First World War but there is very little evidence to support this.

Over on the Wirral, two high explosives landed in a field near Frankby, but no damage was done. Three further high explosives landed in fields near Raby and one near Willaston to much the same effect.

Although nobody would have known it at the time, this was the final raid on Merseyside. An ordeal that had begun 18 months earlier was finally over.

View from St George's Plateau in Liverpool towards the Walker Art Gallery and the County Sessions House in the distance. After the raid on 10 January 1942, air raid shelters like the brick one straight ahead would no longer be needed.

One striking way of demonstrating the effects of the blitz on Merseyside is to show just how long it took to repair some of the damage. The original photograph appeared in Quentin Hughes' book *Seaport* which was first published in the 1960s. At that time, this wartime damage to a corner of the Albert Dock had still not been repaired. It is hard to believe this could be the case now as the Dock is a popular tourist attraction, but it was barely used in the immediate post-war period.

By the late 1970s, Liverpool Docks were in an appalling condition, with the basin filled with mud and the cobblestone floors overgrown. Several schemes were put forward, including some that involved its complete demolition, but common sense prevailed. The dock was eventually regenerated in the early 1980s and became a popular spot, with shops, museums and an art gallery. It was presumably around then that this corner was repaired. Today it remains Britain's largest single group of Grade 1 listed buildings.

The region is full of examples of bomb sites that were either never built on after the war, or were redeveloped fairly recently. Partly this was because of a lack of money, resources and skilled labour in the post-war period. Also, there was just too much damage to ever rebuild everything, so hard decisions had to be made. The legacy of the Blitz is therefore still with us today, and over the next few pages, I will try to show you how you can see this for yourself.

SPOTTING SIGNS OF THE BLITZ

More than seventy years after the raids., you might think that spotting signs of the impact of those far off bombs would prove difficult, at least without a handy reference guide. In many cases, this is correct, for the region has seen massive changes in those seven decades, with whole areas rebuilt to such an extent that they would be unrecognizable to someone who lived through the attacks. There are, however, still signs of the Liverpool Blitz, and these next few pages will take you through some of them.

SIGNS AND PORTENTS

Here and there throughout the region you will occasionally see signs for companies which have long since moved on or shut down. These are known as 'ghost signs' and there is a rather excellent book, *Liverpool Ghost Signs* on the subject by Phil and Caroline Bunford, which includes several wartime examples. One of these is this first sign, found on Eberle Street, which is off Dale Street in Liverpool City Centre.

Although as the Bunfords' book states, this sign looks like it is in too good a condition to be an original, research has since proven that there was indeed a shelter here. It of course indicates an exit from a shelter, in this case in the basement of what was then the premises of the Pioneer Life Assurance Association, which was based at 31 Dale Street. The civil defence workers would find such signs a great help, should they need to rescue people from the building if it collapsed, knowing the location of emergency exits would save crucial minutes. The shelter had room for 104 people.

This second sign comes from a building in Beaconsfield Road, New Ferry which is currently occupied by Andy's Aquatics. It indicates the direction of an Emergency Water Supply site (EWS). Created after the early raids, these supplies could take many forms, including swimming pools, metal tanks and the basements of demolished buildings that had been filled with water. This particular example may refer to the old New Ferry Baths which were in the direction indicated by the arrow. It is probably the best local example of its type to survive.

VISUAL SIGNS OF THE PAST

Often you can tell from looking at a building when it has undergone some reconstruction in the past. Take the example of the building below, which was part of the hydraulic system used in the docks on the Wirral (this building also features on page 24).

You can quite clearly see the difference in colour between the bricks on the left hand corner of the building and the rest. The uneven line running down the wall suggests that this reconstruction wasn't part of a planned rebuild, so it came as no surprise to find that the

building was badly damaged during the blitz, with the damage corresponding almost exactly to the newer brickwork.

Another way is to look for remaining or seemingly older features that look quite out of place with their surroundings or situation. For example, look at the balustrades surrounding the car park in the modern photograph opposite. The feature looks rather unusual and slightly out of place, although not impossible of course given the prominent location (on Victoria Street, the car park is situated behind the Municipal Annexe). A study of the wartime photo however reveals that similar balustrades once surrounded a rather grand structure known as Government Buildings, which was badly damaged and burnt out during the May Blitz. The balustrades seen here are late twentieth-century replacements for the originals.

A NEWER MODEL

You can also often tell when a building has been damaged by a quick comparison of its age and current style. The photo overleaf is of the Bootle Protestant Free Church, which stands on the corner of Trinity Road and University Road. Knowing that a church by the same name appeared in the pre-war street directories reveals that it was probably hit during the raids. This building looks fairly modern and its style is quite likely post-war. Sure enough, the archives contain a photograph of a building of similar layout, but quite different style, with heavy damage to the front of the building and its roof (see page 42). Further research into the air raid records for Bootle revealed that a parachute mine exploded in this area, devastating the church and nearby houses.

MIND THE GAP

Another common way to recognize a blitz site is to look for modern properties or developments that seem incongruous with the rest of the area. One of the first photos I ever investigated was just labelled 'Leopold Street' in the archives.

A visit to the street in question (in Kensington, Liverpool) revealed that it was almost entirely full of terraced housing, with the two notable exceptions (below). Noting their numbers (77 and 79, but there was no 81 or 83), I then matched the names in the street directories for the period to the lists of civilian war dead, and was able to confirm this was the exact location. Four pre-war houses had been demolished and only two rebuilt. Sadly a mother and four daughters had been killed at number 81.

So there we have a quick guide to the kinds of things to look out for on your travels around the Merseyside region. Signs of the Blitz and its impact are all around you, you just need to know where to look.

GLOSSARY

Throughout the course of this book and indeed my previous two titles, various wartime terms are used that may be confusing to anyone not familiar with the period. The following is therefore a quick guide to the more common phrases, abbreviations and names.

Air Raid Precaution (ARP): A crucial part of the civil defence of any region, this organization was dedicated to the safety of civilians during the raids. They issued gas masks, maintained public shelters and organized and policed the blackout. After a raid, they would also attempt to rescue those who were trapped, treat the injured, and search the rubble for survivors.

ARP Controller: A member of the ARP, who was often also a council official. They were responsible for collating information on incidents during a given raid and coordinating the civil defence's response accordingly. They also had the authority to request reinforcements from outside their area if it was deemed necessary.

Anti-Aircraft (AA): A type of artillery designed to shoot down enemy planes. Although not always very effective, they did force German bombers to fly higher, making their aim less accurate. The noise of the guns was a comfort to local people who wanted to know that someone was fighting back.

Anderson Shelter: A small, domed, metal shelter generally buried into the ground and then covered with a thick layer of earth to secure them in place. They had room for up to six people and were generally quite effective. Unfortunately, they were only really available to households with a garden, so had limited use in some parts of the region. They were named after Sir John Anderson.

Auxiliary Fire Service (AFS): A force of fire fighters established in 1938 as part of the government's plan for dealing with air raids. They were organized on a county or borough basis, and although they did a lot of good work, there was a lack of consistency as different areas used different equipment. This made the coordination and the pooling of resources difficult, and it was superseded in 1941 by the National Fire Service.

Barrage Balloon: A large hot air balloon attached to the ground with a strong cable. They were usually placed near important installations such as industrial areas and ports. The cable would damage any enemy bomber which flew into it. They were effective at limiting the use of dive bombers, and for forcing low level bombers to fly higher than they normally would have done.

Blackout: The process of eliminating any form of artificial light during the hours of darkness so that enemy night raiders would find it harder to navigate and target their bombs. In practice, this meant covering windows and doors with paint or heavy curtains, and turning off street lighting. Cars and other vehicles had their headlights directed towards the ground. The blackout was strictly enforced by ARP wardens, with people fined for any transgressions.

Borough: An administrative area, usually a division of a county. Unless otherwise stated, if a reference is made to a borough by name such as Crosby or Birkenhead, it will be the historic wartime one rather than any modern equivalent.

Christmas Blitz: A three-night heavy raid on Merseyside, starting on 20 December 1940. On the fourth night, Manchester was targeted, and badly damaged.

Civil Defence (CD): The overall term for the forces tasked with dealing with the enemy attacks on Britain. They included the ARP, AFS, NFS, fire watchers, police, gas decontamination teams, controllers and messengers.

Emergency Water Supply (EWS): A reserve supply of water, usually stored in tanks, swimming pools, and basements. These were set up as often a lack of water could be a problem after a major raid. Normally the AFS/NFS would use the local water supply, but the bombing often damaged the water mains, cutting off supplies in that area.

Evacuation: The process of moving people from the urban areas to the countryside to get away from the enemy's bombing raids. The original evacuations began before war broke out, with more following when the raids started in earnest. Official evacuations consisted of young children, teachers, disabled people, pregnant women and mothers with very young children. Some unofficial evacuation took place if people had friends or family living in the countryside. Some people also temporarily left the region to stay in the less built up areas during the height of the air raids, returning the next day.

Fire Guard: Also known as fire watchers, they were responsible for guarding a particular building (generally one not occupied at night) and keeping watch for incendiary bombs. They were tasked with reporting any bombs that they saw and dealing with those that fell nearby, often by dumping them in buckets of sand or water. They would generally be expected to fight any small fires using stirrup pumps.

First Aid Party (FAP): A small group of trained individuals who would attend an incident and provide basic medical care on the spot. An important part of their role was also to assess each casualty to determine whether they should be sent home, sent to a first aid post or to a nearby hospital. The staff were often provided or trained by organizations like St John Ambulance.

High Explosive: A type of bomb, typically between 50kg and 1800kg in weight and dropped by enemy bombers. This device was designed to cause blast damage with the aim of demolishing buildings.

Home Guard: A volunteer force of men who were unable to serve in the regular armed forces due to age, infirmity or being in a restricted occupation. This force was originally known as the Local Defence Volunteers and was raised in the aftermath of the Dunkirk evacuation, when fear of a German invasion was at its height. Several local anti-aircraft batteries (including one in Wallasey which fired rockets) were manned by them. At first, it was very poorly equipped, however it provided a useful service throughout the war, before standing down in December 1944 and being disbanded the following year.

Incendiary: A type of bomb, typically smaller in size than most others, so dropped in much larger numbers. The main aim of this type of device was to start a fire where it landed, causing destruction by burning properties out. The smaller types were often easy to counter if they were noticed and dealt with promptly. Some larger types were used as the war went on, including explosive incendiaries.

Incident: The name given to a particular spot where a bomb had exploded or damage was done by some other means such as fire spreading from one building to another.. The ARP would establish an incident post nearby, usually in a building with a phone to make their reports from and summon help if needed.

Luftwaffe: The German Air Force, responsible for the bombing raids on Merseyside during the Second World War. It was commanded by Hermann Goering, a First World War fighter ace. The Luftwaffe was experienced and well-trained, but its bombers were too light to be truly effective. Most of its raids against Merseyside were carried out at night.

March Blitz: A three-night raid, starting on the night of 12 March 1941, which saw particularly heavy damage to both Birkenhead and Wallasey.

May Blitz: A week-long series of raids, beginning on the night of 1 May 1941. This was the darkest period of the bombing for Liverpool, Crosby and Bootle; however, Wallasey and Birkenhead both suffered comparatively little damage. Other raids took place later in May 1941, but this term is normally used to refer to the first week.

Messengers: Quite often during the raids there would be a disruption in communication, which in turn could hinder the civil defence's response to each incident. In recognition of this, a system of messengers was set up, often drawing upon existing youth groups such as the Scouts or Boys' Brigade for members. Initially each branch of the civil defences recruited its own messengers, but in 1941 an official service was established. As a rule, most messengers were young and needed to be fit as they were expected to deliver messages both on foot and by bicycle.

Morrison Shelter: An indoor shelter that resembled a table, consisting of a large metal box with cage-like sides. It was just large enough for a couple to sleep under and was provided mainly to households who did not already have a suitable place in their house to shelter in. They were named after the Minister for Home Security, Herbert Morrison but designed by John Baker, a native of Wallasey.

National Fire Service (NFS): Set up in 1941, the NFS took over the role of fire-fighting by combining the various AFS and regular fire brigades into one large force. It reached its height of 350,000 members in late 1942 and existed until 1948.

Parachute Mine: Ordinarily a naval weapon, (if it landed in water it acted as a normal anti-shipping weapon) this type of device was designed to float to earth, and to explode above ground. The blast effect and radius was much greater than most high explosive bombs. Almost all of the worst incidents of the blitz on Merseyside were caused by one of these devices. Fortunately their size and weight limited the number that an enemy force could drop.

Raid: Generic term for a period of enemy action, generally of a single day or night. Most attacks during the blitz on Merseyside were carried out at night and lasted for several hours, often either side of midnight. A raid will therefore usually have two dates, for example 3-4 May 1941, but for the purposes of the book, we have used the start date.

Raids: Similar to the above, but more generally used, therefore if reference is made to the September raids, this should be interpreted as the damage taking place at some point in that month.

Rest centre: A building converted to help those who were recently made homeless by the air raids. They were usually intended to be only temporary, with people staying there no more than a few nights before moving on to stay with family or friends. Whilst there, they could get food, rest and comfort, all of which were crucial in helping people deal with the dislocation of losing their homes.

Royal Air Force (RAF): The Royal Air Force was one of the major forces involved in the defence of Merseyside during the raids. There were several squadrons based nearby, including a Czechoslovakian unit based in Speke. Night fighters would also operate over the region on some nights.

Salvage Corps: Originally a service founded in 1842 to try and help mitigate the loss of belongings in buildings that had caught fire. During the war, they had close connections to the AFS and NFS, but remained independent of them.

Shelter (other): In addition to Anderson and Morrison shelters, the other three main types were brick built street shelters, trench shelters and large communal shelters. The first of these were especially common in terraced streets, as the lack of gardens made Anderson shelters rare. The second type was often dug in parks or gardens, and were lined with concrete for protection. Communal shelters were generally found under large buildings and were converted from existing crypts, cellars or basements.

Siren: Through a variety of methods (observation, radar, intelligence etc) the authorities would try to obtain as much warning of an impending raid as possible. This would then be communicated to people through the sounding of air raid sirens, a loud dual tone warning sound that would put them on the alert and give time to take shelter. After the raiders had gone, a different sound would be made to signal the all clear and allow people to leave their place of shelter.

Stirrup Pump: A basic type of a fire-fighting device using a pump and bucket of water. It was designed to be manned by three people – one to guide the hose, one to pump the water and one to refill the water. They were often used by fire watchers and ARP wardens.

Unexploded Bomb (UXB): A fairly generic term for any device which had landed but hadn't exploded. These were problematic as the enemy would often drop delayed action bombs, or bombs designed to go off if tampered with or moved. The authorities gradually learnt how to deal with the different types of bomb and fuse, but many brave men lost their lives trying to make a UXB safe.

Warden: A member of the ARP organization. Each warden was responsible for an area near where he lived and was expected to know most of the people who lived there. This would make rescue work much easier, since they would know whether a bombed house was occupied and if so by how many people.

Women's Voluntary Services (WVS): Set up in 1938, their initial task was to assist householders in dealing with the impact of the air raids. Their role was very wide ranging, but generally involved manning and supplying the rest centres and providing food, both to members of the civil defences who were dealing with the aftermath of the raids, and those made homeless by them. After the war they were better known as the Women's Royal Voluntary Services but are now just known as Royal Voluntary Services.

INDEX

Numbers in italics indicate both text and photograph on the page. Text in italics denotes ships. Parenthesis (curved brackets) are used for clarity. Street names are organised in this index by borough.